FAR ABOVE RUBIES

RUBIES

The life of Bethan Lloyd-Jones

LYNETTE G. CLARK

CHRISTIAN
FOCUS

Bethan Lloyd-Jones

Unless otherwise indicated, Scripture quotations are taken from *the Holy Bible, New International Version*®. *NIV*®. Copyright ©1973, 1978, 1984, 2011 by Biblica, Inc.™ Used by permission. All rights reserved worldwide.

Photographs marked with a ¹ are taken with permission from *D.Martyn Lloyd-Jones: The First Forty Years, 1899-1939* and photographs marked with a ² are taken with permission from *David Martyn Lloyd-Jones: The Fight of Faith, 1939-1981*, both written by Iain H. Murray and published by The Banner of Truth Trust banneroftruth.org

Cover photo taken from 'Three generations: Bethan with her mother and Elizabeth' (p.124)

paperback ISBN 978-1-78191-583-7
epub ISBN 978-1-78191-622-3
mobi ISBN 978-1-78191-623-0

Published in 2015
by
Christian Focus Publications Ltd.
Geanies House, Fearn, Ross-shire,
IV20 1TW, Scotland, UK

www.christianfocus.com

Cover design by Daniel van Straaten

Printed by Bell & Bain, Glasgow

CONTENTS

DEDICATION

To my dearest 'girls'—
Rachel and sweetest Arianwen,
Sarah and my darling Nina—
trusting that the Lord will enable us all
in our short lives in this world to
'shine like stars'.

PHILIPPIANS 2:15

ACKNOWLEDGMENTS

This book could never have been written without the help of numerous people. The embryo of the book was a talk on Mrs Lloyd-Jones which I gave at a Christian ladies' conference some years ago. Mrs Elizabeth Catherwood—with her late husband—was kind enough to break into a holiday in Wales to spend a number of hours with me in order to answer questions about her mother, Mrs Lloyd-Jones, and to share certain 'family details'. When I first broached the matter of writing a biography of their mother, both Mrs Catherwood and her younger sister, Ann, were very enthusiastic about this and gave freely of their time on a number of occasions. Much of the information concerning their mother which they shared with me could only have been known by those within the Lloyd-Jones 'nuclear family'. I am deeply indebted to the kindness and hospitality shown to me by these two Christian ladies, and to the encouragement which they gave me. I shall always cherish the memory of time spent with them. Their willingness to share very personal details concerning their mother has, I trust, meant that this book is much more informative and richer in detail than would otherwise have been the case. I am, however, only too conscious of the fact that the pen—or computer, these days—is unable to recreate 'the touch of a vanish'd hand, / And the sound of a voice that is still'. I hope that however feebly I have drawn the portrait of the subject of this book, her daughters will recognise the main features, and that their prayer, which is mine too, will be answered: that the *life* of their mother should be a great blessing to others.

Grandparents have a special relationship with their grand-children. I wish to acknowledge my gratitude to Bethan Lloyd-Jones' grandchildren for sending me their abiding memories of their grandmother. The Christian world owes an incalculable debt to Iain Murray for the many informative, and spiritually enriching and edifying biographies which he has written of various Christian preachers and leaders. His two-volume biography of Dr Lloyd-Jones has been an invaluable source of information on various matters, and I am profoundly grateful to him for giving me permission to use some of the material which he was able to gather from Dr and Mrs Lloyd-Jones while they were still alive. Christopher Catherwood—Mrs Lloyd-Jones' eldest grandchild—filled out Iain Murray's biography with his *Martyn Lloyd-Jones: A Family Portrait*. The book was a pleasure to read, and supplied certain information on *Mrs* Lloyd-Jones which I have incorporated or to which I have alluded. Similarly, Fred Catherwood's *At the Cutting Edge*, an autobiography by Elizabeth's husband, contains further information about Mrs Lloyd-Jones which has found its way into the present book.

Numerous friends of the subject of this book gave generously of their time and supplied additional information which greatly helped me in my writing. I wish to acknowledge especially the help given by the following: Mair Davies (wife of the late Revd J. Elwyn Davies) and her daughter, Mrs Sian Nicholas; Revd Vernon Higham and his wife Morwen; Ceinwen Swann (wife of the late Revd Derek Swann); Eluned Thomas (wife of the late Revd John Thomas); and Majorie Thomas (who attended Bethlehem, Sandfields when Dr Lloyd-Jones was the minister there).

Mrs Lloyd-Jones had a 'gift' and ministry of letter writing. I am very grateful to the Revd Basil Howlett for allowing me to borrow letters which Mrs Lloyd-Jones sent to the Westminster Fellowship of ministers during her years of widowhood. These letters reveal her deep affection and regard for the ministers to whom 'the Doctor' gave himself so unsparingly over the years, and the enormous sense of loss which she continued to experience as a widow. I am also grateful to Awel Irene, niece of the late Mari Jones, for giving me letters and photographs which had belonged to her aunt. I would particularly like to thank Matthew Evans for the enormous help he was to me, in procuring copies of original photographs. He saved me miles of motorway and a tremendous amount of time.

Other friends helped in the writing of this book in different ways. Mrs Enid Jones kindly provided a translation of passages from the biography of Evan Phillips, Mrs Lloyd-Jones' grandfather. Glenys Davies spent many hours translating Welsh letters into English, both on her own and with me at the National Library of Wales. Her husband Gwyn—formerly a Church History lecturer at Wales Evangelical School of Theology—also saved me from one glaring historical inaccuracy in my very first chapter! I shall always be indebted to Glenys for her hard work, and shall treasure the memory of the warm hospitality and fellowship which she and her husband extended to me.

I was so glad to have met Dafydd Ifans, who—Boaz-like!— just *happened* to be in the part of the National Library of Wales where I was working on one of the days I spent there. Dafydd had catalogued all the material belonging to the Lloyd-Jones family, and saved me weeks— or even months—of work in identifying relevant material! Diolch yn fawr, Dafydd.

Certain people supported this project with their prayers. In particular, Graham and Anthea Weale maintained a prayerful interest in the book from the time that I began until it was completed, as did Ann Davies of Bala. My church family at Freeschool Court, Bridgend, will never know how much I was encouraged by their enquiries as to the progress of the work and by their assurance of their prayers for me: 'I thank my God every time I remember you' (Philippians 1:3).

I am deeply indebted to the following at Christian Focus: William Mackenzie (Senior), Willie Mackenzie, Marina Macrae, together with all those whose service for the Lord 'behind the scenes' has meant that the work of moving from manuscript to published book has been a joy and labour of love. Christian Focus has indeed been a wonderful publisher with which to work.

I would indeed have failed if I had not acknowledged my thanks to Dr Rebecca Rine for the numerous helpful recommendations and suggestions which she made. In particular she guided me through the mine-field created by the fact that the U.K. and the U.S. are 'two nations separated by a common language' and thus saved me from employing expressions which may have bewildered American readers. No one could have asked for a more engaging and helpful editor.

Last—but certainly not least—I am profoundly grateful for the help provided by members of my family. My sister, Mrs Susie Humphreys, supplied some material and proposed helpful changes. And what shall I say of my dear husband Stephen? My gratitude and love for him are inestimable. His phenomenal memory has saved me an enormous amount of work and time. I am so thankful for his constant encouragement, his many suggestions and the support he has provided throughout. Without him this book would never have seen the light of day. My daughter Rachel, and her husband Thibault, my son Robert and his wife Sarah, and my youngest son, Roman (David), all urged me to press on when I needed encouragement to persevere.

I am grateful to all the aforementioned for their help. Any inaccuracies or infelicities of style are mine.

Most of all I acknowledge my continual dependence upon the Lord, and wish to record my humble thanks for all His wondrous love and aid.

Thanks be to God for his indescribable gift!
2 Corinthians 9:15

PREFACE

Bethan (pronounced Beth-un) Lloyd-Jones loved her God, her husband, her family, her 'church family', her friends and so many other people with whom she came into contact and whose lives were touched by her fragrant Christian character. She, 'being dead, yet speaks' through her godly example.

You may wonder how this book ever came to be written. I was asked some years ago to speak at a Ladies' Day Conference on the subject, 'The profile of a godly woman'. My own inclination was to choose someone from the eighteenth or nineteenth centuries but my husband suggested that I speak on Bethan Lloyd-Jones, a suggestion which immediately struck a chord within me. Thus began a journey of research into her life, the end result of which is the book that you now hold in your hands. I trust that the life of such a lady may challenge and encourage you, to the extent to which it did me, to live a life consecrated to the Saviour and to his service.

> *Therefore, since we are surrounded by such a crowd*
> *of witnesses, let us throw off everything that hinders*
> *and the sin that so easily entangles, and let us run*
> *with perseverance the race marked out for us. Let*
> *us fix our eyes on Jesus, the author and perfecter of*
> *our faith, who for the joy set before Him endured the*
> *cross, scorning its shame, and sat down at the right*
> *hand of the throne of God. Consider Him … so that*
> *you will not grow weary and lose heart.*
> HEBREWS 12:2–3

FAMILY TREE – PHILLIPS

selected family members

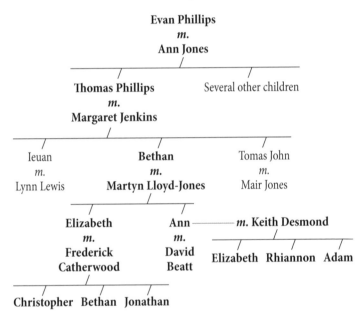

Evan Phillips
m.
Ann Jones

Thomas Phillips
m.
Margaret Jenkins

Several other children

Ieuan
m.
Lynn Lewis

Bethan
m.
Martyn Lloyd-Jones

Tomas John
m.
Mair Jones

Elizabeth
m.
Frederick Catherwood

Ann
m.
David Beatt

m. **Keith Desmond**

Elizabeth   Rhiannon   Adam

Christopher   Bethan   Jonathan

PROLOGUE:
A SMILE IN PLACE OF TEARS

A wife of noble character who can find?
Proverbs 31:10

If Jesus Christ be God and died for me, then no sacrifice
can be too great for me to make for him.
C.T. Studd

Giving … to God

*One morning, after breakfast, when he was preparing to go out on
one of his long journeys, the room looked so bright and cosy that a
sudden depression seized me at the thought of its emptiness when he
was gone, and the many anxious hours that must pass before I should
see him again. Some tears would trickle down my cheeks, in spite of
my efforts to restrain them. Seeing me look so sad, he said, very gently,
'Wifey, do you think that, when any of the children of Israel brought
a lamb to the Lord's altar as an offering to him, they stood and wept
over it when they had seen it laid there?' 'Why, no!' I replied, startled
by his strange question, 'certainly not; the Lord would not have been
pleased with an offering reluctantly given'. 'Well,' he said tenderly,
'don't you see, you are giving me to God, in letting me go to preach
the gospel to poor sinners, and do you think he likes to see you cry
over your sacrifice?' Could ever a rebuke have been more sweetly*

and graciously given? It sank deep into my heart, carrying comfort with it, and, thenceforward, when I parted with him, the tears were scarcely ever allowed to show themselves, or if a stray one or two dared to run over the boundaries, he would say, 'What! crying over your lamb, wifey!' and this reminder would quickly dry them up, and bring a smile in their place.[1]

—Susannah Spurgeon

The influence for good of the preaching and written ministry of C.H. Spurgeon—in being used both to bring people to faith in Christ and then to nurture that faith—has been incalculable. But behind his remarkable ministry was a devoted woman who was willing, as the above quotation makes clear, to make sacrifices— 'giving up her lamb'—for the work of God's kingdom.

In many ways, the ministry of Martyn Lloyd-Jones bears comparison with that of Spurgeon. The influence of his powerful evangelistic and expository preaching; his extensive travels and labours in the cause of Christ; his fearless commitment to biblical truth: in all these areas there are striking similarities, as well as some significant differences, between 'the Doctor' and Spurgeon. The subject of this book, however, is not Dr Lloyd-Jones but his wife: for, just as Susannah Spurgeon 'gave up her lamb' to the Lord, so, throughout her married life, did Bethan Lloyd-Jones. There are women as well as men in the gallery of the great heroes of faith; although not placed in as prominent a position for all to see, their service has been invaluable in God's kingdom.

The wife of Dr Lloyd-Jones was such a woman. Her portrait has long been hidden in a part of the gallery known only to her family and certain close friends. Their humility and proper modesty have been such that there the portrait might well have remained in relative obscurity. But a life so devoted to the honour of Jesus Christ and to the glory of His name—a devotion which often shone through in the little and unseen things—is a witness to the

---

1. Spurgeon (1962), 418.

power of godliness and has much to teach us. It is for this reason, with the full agreement of her daughters, that I am placing her portrait in a 'public place'.

In his definitive biography of Dr Martyn Lloyd-Jones, Iain Murray noted that the Doctor 'lived in several worlds at once'.[2] To a greater or lesser degree this, of course, is true of all people—Mrs Lloyd-Jones included. It is inevitable that immediate family members will have the privilege of seeing aspects of someone's personality, character, interests, likes and dislikes that are denied to those outside the family circle. Close friends will also know things about a person that mere acquaintances can never know. In writing of someone who is survived by those who knew them intimately, there will always be the danger that a biographer will leave the reader with a somewhat different impression of the subject from that of those who knew the person well. This can be so even in those cases, such as the present, where the immediate surviving family members—in this instance, Mrs Lloyd-Jones' two daughters—have freely shared information, some of which was hitherto known only to the family. I am acutely aware that a biography can never take the place of the person herself, and this is certainly so in the present case: a portrait, after all, is not the same as the living person. But portraits—and biographies—serve a unique purpose. One may, for example, study aspects of a character's face in a portrait gallery in a way that would be singularly inappropriate when sitting across from the living person!

Godliness is something more easily seen 'fleshed out' in a real person than studied in the abstract. For this reason, whatever deficiencies there may be in the 'word portrait' which I have painted—and for which I now crave the reader's indulgence—I put it in a public place that the reader may worship the God of all grace who produced such a fragrantly godly life, and be stirred to emulate those whose faith we are called to follow.

---

2. Murray (1990), 754.

1

OPEN HOMES AND OPEN HEARTS

You have given me the heritage of those who fear your name.
<small>PSALM 61:5b</small>

*Our Father refreshes us on the journey with some
pleasant inns, but will not encourage us
to mistake them for home.*
<small>C.S. LEWIS</small>

ANCESTRY

Powerful preachers

Cadair Idris is one of the most striking mountains in North
Wales, situated near the towns of Machynlleth and Dolgellau.
Legend has it that if someone spends a night asleep on it, they
will awake the next morning as either a poet or a madman![1]
Christmas Evans was neither of these, though he was certainly
possessed of the imaginative gift of the poet. Born in South Wales
in 1766 and 'born again' while a young man, he was to become
a preacher of extraordinary power in North Wales, planting
churches in what is known as the Lleyn Peninsula and on the

---

1. See www.visitsnowdonia.info/myths_and_legends-89.aspx.

island of Anglesey. He became involved, however, in a bitter religious controversy for about five years and lost his joy in the Lord and his spiritual usefulness. It was while he was travelling on a lonely road near Cadair Idris that he had an encounter with God which restored him and led to renewed blessing in his ministry. From his diary we have a description of what happened that day:

> I was weary of a cold heart towards Christ, and his sacrifice and the work of his Spirit—of a cold heart in the pulpit, in secret prayer, and in the study ... On a day ever to be remembered by me, as I was going from Dolgellau to Machynlleth and climbing up towards Cadair Idris, I considered it incumbent upon me to pray, however hard I felt my heart, and however worldly the frame of my spirit was. Having begun in the name of Jesus, I soon felt as it were the fetters loosening, and the old hardness of heart softening, and, as I thought, mountains of frost and snow dissolving and melting within ... I felt my whole mind relieved from some great bondage: tears flowed copiously, and I was constrained to cry out for the gracious visits of God, by restoring to my soul the joy of his salvation ... This struggle lasted for three hours; it rose again and again, like one wave after another, or a high flowing tide driven by a strong wind, until my nature became faint by weeping and crying. Thus I resigned myself to Christ, body and soul, gifts and labours—all my life—every day and every hour that remained for me:—and all my cares I committed to Christ.[2]

The effect of this experience on his preaching was soon to be felt by the people. Like Cyclops of old he had but one eye, but that eye could transfix vast congregations as he preached simply and graphically. Multitudes were spellbound and moved to the

---

2. Shenton (2001), 179–80.

depths of their being as he brought his powerful imagination to bear upon the truths of Scripture, which he proclaimed with such singular effect.

But what link did this powerful Welsh preacher of the nineteenth century have with the wife of another Welshman, who was one of the greatest preachers of the twentieth century? While God's grace and salvation do not 'run in the blood', there is, nevertheless, such a thing as 'the heritage of those who fear the Lord', and Bethan Lloyd-Jones was blessed with such a heritage. Her great-great-grandfather was a cousin of Christmas Evans: to be precise, he was a first cousin twice removed.[3]

Although Evan Phillips did not exercise the same measure of spiritual influence as Christmas Evans, he was, nevertheless, a godly man and powerful preacher, and was certainly every bit as colourful a character as his illustrious relative. It is with Evan Phillips that we shall begin to trace the family background and the varied influences for good which helped to mould the godly lady whose portrait we are to study.

Family life was very happy

Evan Phillips was born in 1829, and he married Ann Jones in 1859. In 1860 he was ordained a minister in the Welsh Calvinistic Methodist Church, and later that year he became the minister of Bethel Chapel, Newcastle Emlyn, in Cardiganshire. He was a preacher of considerable ability and power:

> ... [he was] one of the great preachers of his age. His ideas were so fresh and sparkling, his pictures so natural, and his eloquence so persuasive that the 'twenty-minute preacher' won a very special place for himself. His sermons were characterised by a combination of the poet's imagination, the teacher's acumen, and the evangelical's ardour.[4]

---

3. See Appendix 1.

4. See The National Library of Wales, Phillips.

This is high praise indeed for someone who lived at a time when Wales was blessed with numerous powerful preachers. It would seem that the gift of the poet's imagination, which had so animated Christmas Evans' sermons, ran in the blood of this family. A graphic way of preaching was something which characterised both of these ministries. And, as we shall see, a vivid imagination was something which Bethan Lloyd-Jones inherited from the Phillips side of her ancestry.

Evan Phillips and his wife Ann were blessed with eight children. Evan was devoted to his family—so devoted, in fact, as to lead on occasion to somewhat amusing, if not downright eccentric, behaviour on his part. When he went from home to preach, although reluctant to leave his family behind, he was always ready a good hour before the appointed time, and he would then expect all the family to help him on his way and to escort him to the railway station. A wife and eight children traipsing from the house to the station would have been quite an affair! But his devotion to his family was such that, when he was away preaching, it was certainly not a case of 'out of sight, out of mind', but much more one of 'absence makes the heart grow fonder'. Evan Phillips was not just reluctant to leave home; he was sometimes disinclined to stay at the places that he visited when he actually arrived there. On numerous occasions he insisted on having a meeting in a church at which he was a visiting preacher moved from 6 p.m. to 3 p.m. so that he could return home earlier! At least on these occasions he stayed for the afternoon meeting. But there were times when the congregation was to be disappointed:

> *Whenever Evan Phillips was absent from home he had a 'hiraeth' (longing) to return. On several occasions we discover he left the place he was preaching at, to return home, as his 'hiraeth' was so intense … We read that when he was preaching on a certain occasion in Liverpool—one of the children, where he was staying, began to sing, 'Home Sweet*

Home'—he instantly fetched his coat and said, 'I'm going home, I can't stay here a moment longer!'[5]

It was not that he was anxious about his family. Quite the contrary! He was always concerned for his children, but confessed that when he was away from home he 'gave them up to God' and had no concern for them whatsoever because he knew God cared for them more than he could ever do so. It was simply that he loved to be with his family. And it is evident that his family life was very happy indeed. Something of the atmosphere of the home in which Bethan Phillips' father was nurtured was, in turn, to pervade the home in which he would bring up his children, and this was to be carried on when Bethan became Mrs Lloyd-Jones.

In Ann Jones, Evan Phillips found a wife who was truly of noble character and who complemented him well. She was endowed with a very practical nature. She is described by her husband's biographer as being of strong character, tender, distinguished and humble. She was very caring for all the poor in the neighbourhood and always turned a deaf ear to any gossip. And Ann, like her husband, loved her home more than anywhere else—so it is just as well she did not have to leave in order to preach!

If Evan could be somewhat eccentric, then it also has to be said that Ann's way of supporting and encouraging her husband was sometimes unconventional. On one occasion, Evan was very loath to leave home and to preach at Carmarthen, though the reason had nothing to do with a reluctance to leave his family; rather, he was convinced that if he went, he would return in his coffin! One wonders if he was suffering from a touch of the hypochondria to which—as Dr Lloyd-Jones would later claim—preachers are

---

5. Morgan (1930), 63. It is worth noting that Bethan Lloyd-Jones was not altogether happy with J.J. Morgan's biography of Evan Phillips. As we shall see, she spent numerous holidays with him when she was a child, and, according to her daughter Elizabeth, she felt that the biography did not give a full representation of her grandfather.

particularly prone. If he was, his wife soon encouraged him to think differently: she said he could not disappoint the congregation and that, since the people of Carmarthen should not be put to any expense, the best thing to do would be to call for the undertaker to get Evan measured up for a coffin before he left! Needless to say, he fulfilled the preaching engagement. This concern about his health could sometimes lead him to take drastic measures. His biographer gives an amusing example:

> … [he was] prone to bouts of depression and melancholy. When two of his close friends died the same week Evan Phillips became convinced that he would die. He retired to his bed to meditate on the brevity of life and the emptiness of men's hope. 'Two have gone,' he groaned, 'there is bound to be a third—and that will be me.' This was his constant cry. One morning Mrs Phillips went out to feed the pigs. She noticed that one had died. Immediately she shouted to her husband, 'Evan, the third has died, you are safe to come down now!!' He left his bed![6]

Ann Phillips was clearly a shrewd and sensible lady, who knew how best to handle her husband. He laid great store by his wife's judgment, particularly where it concerned his preaching. On one particular Saturday evening he confided in her, with great concern, that he had nothing to give to his people the next day—truly, a preacher's nightmare. She replied that she was not sure that he ever had anything to say! Although this upset him, it must have been the very thing he needed to hear, because the next day he preached with great liberty and power. On another occasion she asked Evan to explain to her what exactly he had given to the people after a morning meeting. Before he could answer, she said, 'If you have no better for this evening, I would advise you to stay at home so that they can have a prayer meeting!'

---

6. ibid., 68.

Although the medicine Ann administered to her husband was acerbic, it is clear that her concern was the well-being of the people. Thus on another occasion she asked him, 'Do you really think that the people will be sustained till next week on the basis of tonight's sermon?'[7] The question—asked in the 1880s—is a revealing one, and bespeaks an attitude to the ministry of God's Word which would be shared by Bethan Lloyd-Jones' husband in the next century. Since this was something which was so central to Dr Lloyd-Jones' conception of preaching; and since, like her grandmother, Mrs Lloyd-Jones sought to help her husband in his ministry—'My work is to keep him in the pulpit', she would sometimes say—it will be profitable briefly to explore what lay behind Ann Phillips' question to her husband.

For some today, preaching is little more than an exposition of a verse or passage of Scripture: the text is explained, and is then applied by drawing out lessons for belief and behaviour in the contemporary world. The thinking behind Ann Phillips' question was that preaching, while never less than this, was to be much more: it was to feed and nourish the soul from one week to another. Thus, if people were illiterate and could not read the Scriptures for themselves or if they were too poor to possess their own copy of the Scriptures, they could ruminate throughout the week on what they had heard on Sunday. Furthermore—and this was the emphasis which Dr Lloyd-Jones maintained throughout his ministry—the task of preaching is not simply to *inform* but to *transform*. One of the ways in which this was to be achieved was by *stirring* the people's affections, so that the effect of the message will be to stimulate appetite within them for the Word of God.[8]

---

7. ibid., 67.

8. Lloyd-Jones (1976), 112. He says: 'The primary object of preaching is not only to give information. It is, as Edwards says, to produce an impression. It is the impression at the time that matters, even more than what you can remember subsequently...Edwards, in my opinion, has the true notion of preaching. It is not primarily to impart information: and while you are

Ann Phillips perfectly understood the complexities of her husband's personality. Her presence in the church services was vital to him. The observation was made that Evan did not attain great heights in respect to his preaching when she was absent! She was exactly the kind of wife needed for a man with his vivid imagination and of such a nervous disposition. She provided balance in the face of his extremes. One can only surmise that had she not been the critic and spur to him that he found her to be, it is unlikely that his preaching would have had the impact which it did. This having been said, she clearly lacked the diplomatic touch which, we shall see later, Mrs Lloyd Jones possessed when assessing her husband's ministry. 'The Doctor' was to refer to her as 'my best critic'. *How* something is said can be as important as *what* is said: 'A word aptly spoken is like apples of gold in settings of silver' (Prov. 25:11, NIV 2003).

One thing which certainly characterised Evan Phillips' household was a care and generosity towards other people: if Evan and Ann Phillips loved their family, they were not absorbed with their family to the exclusion of others. They loved to entertain God's servants, and there was always a meal at hand for any who passed by. Evan's salary was very small—just £15 per annum—but they were fortunate that his wife's family were comfortably placed and contributed to their needs. The Phillipses were very generous with all that they had, and we will see this characteristic in Tom Phillips, Bethan's father, who had grown up in this atmosphere of love and open-handedness. We are told that later in life the Phillips children found it hard to leave their home and that Dr Tom Phillips never departed without tears. But leave he did, travelling to London in the 1890s to make his way in the big city. There he met and married Margaret Jenkins.

---

writing your notes you may be missing something of the impact of the Holy Spirit. As preachers we must not forget this. We are not merely imparters of information ... what we need above everything else today is moving, passionate, powerful preaching. It must be "warm" and it must be "earnest."

The distinguished 'London Welsh'

Bethan was born to Thomas and Margaret Phillips on 19 May 1898, the same day that Gladstone died,[9] which also happened to be Ascension Day. Thomas Phillips became a deacon at Charing Cross Welsh Calvinistic Methodist Chapel. Prior to this they had attended another Welsh chapel, during which time Bethan was born. The family was one of the distinguished 'London Welsh' who had made their way in the capital city. They lived comfortably in Harrow, a London suburb: the house had a tennis court and the family had kitchen staff and a gardener.

Dr Phillips was an eminent ophthalmologist or eye specialist. One of his patients was fellow Welshman David Lloyd George, who would become the British Prime Minister from 1916–1922. Although he had patients and friends who were drawn from the upper echelons of society—and when Bethan was born, British society was far more stratified along 'class' lines than it is today—Tom Phillips always had time for those from the 'lower' end of the social scale and for those whose lives had been ravaged by time and bad fortune. Much of his work was done amongst those who were too poor to pay, and he was always ready to help those in need.

One evening while attending the chapel, Bethan's father noticed, at the end of the meeting, an elderly lady in the front row weeping profusely. When he enquired into her distress, he found that she had been dismissed from her employment as a cook on the grounds that she was too old: she had been in service to this family for forty years! She felt utterly bereft, having no family and no reason to return to her homeland of Wales. Without hesitation, Tom Phillips took Miss Jones home to become his family's cook, and she lived with them for many years. In his own words, 'She was a boon and blessing to the family'. On another occasion, he found a fellow Welshman who was unemployed, drunk and in the gutter,

---

9. William Ewart Gladstone served the British Government in four terms of office as Prime Minister: 1868–1874, 1880–1885, February–July 1886, and 1892–1894.

with nowhere to live. He too was taken to the Phillips' home and became their gardener. This bigheartedness of her father—which he had learned from his own father—was a wonderful example to Bethan, and in later years was to be the pattern of her own life.

Mr Phillips was to play a significant part in the life of Martyn Lloyd-Jones. Bethan's father encouraged open debate in his adult Sunday School class, which Martyn attended from 1917–1924, and such good-natured friendly discussion between the two men probably continued when Martyn married into the family some years later.

Bethan's mother had been a school teacher. She was a fine Christian, although a somewhat private individual. However, this did not prevent her from operating an 'open house policy'. Elizabeth can think of at least four nephews and nieces, as well as many other individuals, who needed help at one time or another and whom were taken into the home by her grandmother. We know that early in her life she held to the Keswick 'higher life' teaching.[10] Margaret Phillips was a very clever woman and quite advanced and ahead of her time in her thinking: she, like Thomas, believed that girls should be as well educated as boys—a belief which, in the West, we take for granted today but which, in those days, was not at all a widely held idea. Margaret's closest friends were dairy owners. Both Elizabeth and Ann remember being behind the counter at their grandparents' shop. Many of the Cardiganshire Welsh owned dairies in London, collecting the milk at Paddington railway station early in the morning—Dr Lloyd-Jones remembered these 'crack of dawn' experiences. There is a very interesting book on this subject, *Cows, Cardies and Cockneys*,[11] which was written about these London Welsh dairy owners. A considerable number of the Carmarthenshire Welsh present in the city owned the drapers shops, preferring them to the dairies. Many of these families

10. Keswick is a place in the Lake District (England) where Conventions were held for 'the deepening of the spiritual life', which was referred to as the 'deeper life' or the 'higher life'.

11. Jones (1984).

from both these regions of Wales attended Charing Cross Chapel. Margaret as well as her husband was involved in the life of the Chapel. Bethan's mother taught a large Sunday School class that was a Bible-based ministry to women of all ages.

Bethan had two brothers, to whom she was very close: Ieuan, who was two years older than her, and Tomos John, who was six years her junior. Ieuan would later become a minister at Neath in South Wales, and Tomos John would follow in his father's steps as an eye specialist in London.

CHILDHOOD EXPERIENCES

Revival and the extraordinary

When Bethan was six and Ieuan eight years old, their father sent them to their grandparents' home in Newcastle Emlyn: a spiritual revival was taking place in Wales at this time,[12] and Tom Phillips wanted his children to savour something of the spiritual atmosphere which was prevalent in his parents' home and church. Mrs Phillips had initially expressed reservations about this because of the effect upon their education of being absent from school. Years later, Bethan recounted the conversation between her mother and father:

'Maggie, … I'm determined that we should send Ieuan and Bethan down to Newcastle Emlyn—now, at once.'

---

12. This was what is known as 'The 1904 Welsh Revival'. It is undoubtedly the case that this revival was more 'mixed' than earlier revivals in Wales. As a result it has tended to have occasioned more disagreement and controversy amongst evangelicals and those who are positive about the whole concept of revival than is the case with other revivals. Furthermore, there have not been wanting those who have argued that its effects were short-lived. However, though 'mixed', it is nevertheless the case that there was a genuine and extensive work of God, however much this may have been disfigured by certain excesses. For accounts which draw attention to both the reality of God's work at that time and to its long-term effects, as well as to the excesses, see Evans (1987) and Clark (2004).

'But Tom bach,[13] *why? What on earth for? And anyway, what about school?'*

'Maggie, they can go to school anytime, but perhaps they may never again see revival.'[14]

Although they would make the journey on many occasions with their parents from London to their grandparents' home in Newcastle Emlyn, on this occasion they were sent on their own from Paddington Station to make the journey. Those, of course, were different days from ours. It is unlikely that children would travel this route unaccompanied today. The guard was given half-a-crown—just over twelve pence, which was quite a lot of money in those days—to look after the two youngsters. Eighty-three years later, Bethan could still remember the feeling of anxiety as she saw her father disappear from view. He was reported as saying that the most important thing he ever did in his life was to send his children to Newcastle Emlyn at that time. Successful professional man though he was, this statement reveals where his true priorities lay.

Certainly it was not only the feeling of anxiety at seeing her father recede from her view at Paddington Station which stayed with her throughout life. Other events that occurred while staying with her grandparents left an indelible mark on her memory. In particular, she witnessed some of the extraordinary phenomena which might occur in revival.

One fascinating incident concerned the behaviour of Evan Roberts, who spent some time at the home of Bethan's grandparents while she and Ieuan were there. Roberts was a young man who had been studying at a preparatory school for those who were to enter the theological college of the Welsh Calvinistic Methodist Church to train for its ministry. The head of the school was Bethan's

---

13. 'Bach' is the Welsh word for 'little', but it is also used as a term of endearment.

14. Lloyd-Jones (1987), 9.

uncle, Tomos John. Roberts had, however, abandoned this training to return to his home area to hold meetings,[15] and before long remarkable things were happening, with numerous people coming to living faith in Jesus Christ. Although there were undoubtedly aspects of Evan Roberts' behaviour which one may legitimately question and criticise, it would be quite wrong to regard him—as some have—as no more than a wide-eyed fanatic.[16] Bethan's family themselves sometimes had reservations about a number of Roberts' actions, but invariably, subsequent events led them to revise their adverse judgments. Bethan remembered one vivid incident concerning him at this time:

Very early one morning … There was a knock at the Sunnyside door … There stood a weary young man, looking dishevelled, somewhere in his late teens. He sounded desperate and unhappy, as he said he must see Evan Roberts. Auntie Ann … told him of the early caller, and of his desperate and pitiful appearance. The answer was unequivocal: 'Ann, I can't see him. I have no freedom to do so' … Now, she was as desperate as the young man, and she could not help pleading with him … 'Oh Evan, can't you give me some word, some message for him?' 'Yes, I can do that—tell him to read Psalm 27, verse 10.' She was back with the young man in a moment. No, Evan Roberts could not see him, but, 'he has sent you a message. You are to read Psalm 27, verse 10.' There lay the Bible on the table … as he read, according to Auntie Ann, his misery vanished and he shed tears of joy in his amazement and relief. The verse read: 'When my father and my mother forsake me, then the Lord will take me up.' When he could speak he told her his

---

15. Although this was an unusual step to take, it is not without significance that Evan Phillips encouraged Roberts in this, believing that God's hand was upon him in an unusual way. For further reading on this, see Clark (2004), 69–91.

16. Evans (1987) and Clark (2004).

story. He was from Lampeter—about 30 miles from Newcastle Emlyn. The previous night he had been to a meeting in his home church and had come under a tremendous pressure of the Holy Spirit present in that meeting. He had been gloriously converted and, in the joy of that experience, had gone home to tell his parents. He had been met, not by joy, not by indifference or mockery, but by concentrated fury from his parents. They would have none of it, and finally delivered their ultimatum: he must give it all up or go. They had literally turned him out late at night with nowhere to go ... he had walked the 30 miles through the night from Lampeter ... nobody had known anything about him. God alone could have revealed his problem to Evan Roberts and moved his servant to give him such a message of comfort and reassurance. So he went, not knowing where he was going, but knowing that 'He who has led will lead ...' and that, though his earthly parents had forsaken him, 'the Lord had taken him up'.[17]

Bethan's family had first-hand knowledge of Evan Roberts and of what sometimes seemed to them his strange behaviour. But, as Bethan observed in later life:

This unquestioning heed and obedience to an unmistakable inner authority came to be recognised by all who knew Evan in those days, especially perhaps by the family at Sunnyside. At times, they thought he was going too far or was unreasonable or, indeed, unkind, in the things he refused to do. Yet they inevitably found that he was right and showed a prescience and wisdom far beyond any human capacity at the time. They learned to accept his decisions and to acknowledge them as obedience to God's will.[18]

---

17. Lloyd-Jones (Oct. 1987), 10.

18. ibid., 10. Of course, such an approach could lead to excess, and it is indisputable that at times Roberts carried this too far. Dr Lloyd-Jones—who knew Roberts—commented on this on numerous occasions. See his

It was not only Evan Robert's actions that stayed in Bethan's memory. She recalls a special moment when her brother—a mere eight years of age—took part in a prayer meeting:

> I don't recall a word he said, but he was pouring out his heart and looking radiant. He never hesitated for a word, but went on—and on—and on. I thought that one or two of the deacons were beginning to look anxious. However, my grandfather, the minister ... tapped him gently on the shoulder and said: 'All right, my boy, all right.' This little eight year old, unruffled and obedient, sat down quietly and the prayer meeting went on. I remember telling Martyn about that incident once, and he said: 'You know, even now, when Ieuan is praying, I sometimes hear a note of those days in his prayer.'[19]

Being sent to the scenes of revival at Newcastle Emlyn had a profound and lasting effect upon Mrs Lloyd-Jones. Her mature assessment is revealing:

> The revival was no flash in the pan. We were seeing, every day of our lives, the reality of unseen spiritual things. Nothing ever took that away from us ... When we went home to Harrow, our cousin Dilys, then twelve years old (to our eight and six), came to stay with us for a while. We three had prayer meetings ... Dilys was truly converted and had a good spiritual understanding, and was a great leader for our little meetings. She would read short passages from the Bible to us and she made sure that we never thought of these meetings as a game ... The revival had spread to the Welsh churches in London, with the same tremendous impact.[20]

'Foreword to Evans', where he refers to the tendency of Roberts to cross a line from the spiritual into the psychic. See also Clark (2004).

19. Lloyd-Jones (Sept. 1987), 10.

20. ibid., 11.

These early beginnings were a great spiritual back-drop to her life.

In later life Bethan would find herself in the midst of scenes of considerable spiritual blessing under her husband's ministry. She would also, on occasion, experience unusual episodes of prescience to which we shall later refer. Her time spent as a six year old, in the midst of revival, was undoubtedly one of the most valuable experiences of her life. How right her father had been in his decision to send Bethan and her brother to witness true revival!

'Sunnyside'

Bethan loved her grandparents and was always thrilled to be at Newcastle Emlyn. One of her early memories of such a visit was of her rushing through the passageway into the loving arms of her 'Mamo' (grandmother) or one of her aunts. She felt 'enveloped' in love at Sunnyside and had such fond memories of the times that were spent there. The house was always full of people: someone once said, 'It was like a public house without the beer!'[21] The deep impression of the love which the extended family had for one another stayed with Bethan all her days. This is how, in old age, she spoke of the excitement which she experienced in going to Newcastle Emlyn:

We made that trip so often that these memories moved into the familiar pattern of our young lives—the arrival, the wait for the train to stop, the exit with bags in hand, the handing over of tickets, then a top speed dash to Sunnyside. Sometimes … the little one-horse bus was there and, if he was not engaged and without a fare, the driver would give us a ride to the door—sheer joy! At other times, if we were expected, there would always be an Uncle—usually Uncle Jack—to meet us and walk down with us. At the railings outside the door of

---

21. Lloyd-Jones (Oct. 1987), 10.

Sunnyside every available member of the family would be there to greet us.[22]

Bethan and her family were regular visitors at Sunnyside—they visited at least two or three times a year for holidays. Back in London was much the same: a very happy place, overflowing with visitors. The Phillips' home was once described by Bethan, in later years, as 'the house that none-go-by'. Such open, loving homes obviously had an effect on Bethan Phillips, as they had done on her father and her mother before her: in years to come she would open not only her home but also her heart to many of God's people.

Offer hospitality to one another without grumbling. Each one should use whatever gift he has received to serve others.
1 PETER 4:9–10

---

22. Lloyd-Jones (Sept. 1987),9.

Bethan and her brother Ieuan.

Sunnyside(left), Newcastle Emlyn.[1]

Bethan with her father and mother (Dr Tom and Mrs Margaret Phillips).[1]

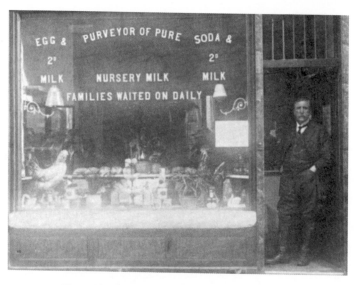

Henry Lloyd-Jones at the door of his dairy business,
Regency Street, Westminster.[1]

2

GIVEN ... A SORT OF GIFT

Charm is deceptive, and beauty is fleeting:
But a woman who fears the LORD is to be praised.
PROVERBS 31:30

A beautiful woman delights the eye; a wise woman, the
understanding; a pure one, the soul.
MINNA ANTRIM

Her beauty and intellect

A woman was once heard to say of her children: 'They say you can't have beauty and brains, but my children have the lot!' She was hardly the most modest of women, nor was she possessed of good or refined taste to make such a remark. By contrast, Bethan Lloyd-Jones was naturally modest and unassuming, and this modesty would later be sanctified and refined by God's Spirit, making her a woman who was truly clothed with humility. She would never have said such a thing of herself, nor would her parents: it is, however, a simple fact that she was, from her youth, and even into her old age, an unmistakably beautiful woman who was also possessed of considerable intelligence. It seems that her good looks were inherited from her father's side of the family: he was very striking in appearance. However, her mother certainly was not plain: she had been considered quite pretty when she was younger.

In our celebrity-obsessed culture, female beauty is something which is idolised and worshipped, but Bethan had a far more down-to-earth and common sense approach to her good looks. As far as she was concerned, 'I thought God had given me a sort of gift, like being told you have lovely blue eyes or that you are tall.' Even before she had come to personal faith in Christ as her Saviour, God's common grace enabled her to see that physical beauty was not a personal achievement in which to boast but simply one of God's good gifts.

As we shall see, Bethan's 'good looks' caused many heads to turn and would lead to many proposals of marriage, but her beauty never turned her own head. Bethan's elder daughter, Elizabeth, relates how people often asked her how she found growing up with such a gifted and well-known preacher as her father. Her response was that in some respects she regarded it far more 'difficult' having such a beautiful mother.

Her education

Intelligence and intellectual ability need to be trained and disciplined: education is surely about far more than acquiring certain skills or 'cramming' to pass exams. Education is concerned with developing a person's gifts and drawing out latent abilities from within, producing a well-rounded personality and character. Bethan's parents certainly believed in the value of her having a good education: her father made enquiries from some of his well-connected friends as to which school would be best for his very gifted daughter. After leaving primary school, she won a scholarship to the North London Collegiate School—a very prestigious academy.

Part of the weekly ritual in her school was the learning and reciting of poetry. The learning of a lengthy poem was rewarded with 'points', which could be collected. Robert Browning was one of her favourite poets. He had not long died and was regarded as one of the 'moderns' of her time. Bethan carried many a prize book from the school podium on account of her ability in English literature. Years later her elder daughter, Elizabeth, recalled her mother's ritual:

> *Mother loved poetry, and because of the wonderful education she received at the North London Collegiate School, she could quote screeds of it. I remember being transfixed as a little girl when, as she was drying my hair in front of the fire one evening, she recited 'The Forsaken Merman' by Matthew Arnold from beginning to end.*[1]

Although she loved literature, throughout her school years Bethan had always been interested in the medical profession, having a great desire to do good to her fellow men and women. And so it was that, on leaving school, she took up medical studies at University College, London. (It was an interesting coincidence that her husband-to-be began studying medicine on the very same day at St Bartholomew's Hospital, London.) The year was 1916: a time when few women were accepted to train as doctors—in fact, there had only been one other intake of women students reading medicine prior to her starting her course. She obtained her degree at the University and became a Member of the Royal College of Surgeons (M.R.C.S.; L.R.C.P.). However, like her father, she was quite self-effacing with respect to her achievements and was totally devoid of pride and pomposity about them. Her father's spirituality safeguarded him from snobbery and although still not a Christian, Bethan Phillips was kept, by common grace, from arrogance.

> *For you created my inmost being;*
> > *you knit me together in my mother's womb.*
> *I praise you because I am fearfully and wonderfully made;*
> > *your works are wonderful,*
> > *I know that full well ...*
> *All the days ordained for me were written in your book*
> > *before one of them came to be.*
>
> PSALM 139:13–14, 16b

1. Lady Elizabeth Catherwood. *A letter to the author.*

Bethan, aged about eighteen, in Welsh costume.[1]

3

LOVE IS MORE THAN SKIN DEEP

Let love and faithfulness never leave you;
bind them around your neck,
write them on the tablet of your heart.
Then you will win favour and a good name
in the sight of God and man.
PROVERBS 3:3–4

Life is a succession of lessons which must be
lived to be understood.
HELEN KELLER

Society life

Given her upbringing and social status, Bethan could easily have become little more than a socialite. As a young woman, she was frequently invited to fashionable house parties in the country, mostly connected with friends from the church. She could set a dinner party alight with her strong views. Perhaps this is why Martyn and she had so many disagreements when they first became friendly with one another.

The circles in which the Phillipses moved were such that there was regular social contact between the family members and people of eminence and influence. We have already had occasion to observe that the family was acquainted with David Lloyd George. The man who had been British Prime Minister during part of World War I when Britain still had a considerable empire, and who had been involved in the events leading to the Treaty of Versailles in 1919 (however adverse the verdict of history upon aspects of his character and leadership might be) was evidently a man who was very much at the centre of things. Although he fell from office in 1922 and was 'a political pariah for the rest of his life',[1] the fact that he was a friend of the family gives some idea of the circles in which the Phillips family moved. (The wedding present he gave them, a beautiful coffee jug with accompanying cups and saucers, is still in the family.) It also testifies to the fact that the Phillipses did not shun those who had fallen from favour in the eyes of others.

The first time Bethan saw Martyn was in the late summer of 1914 in Charing Cross Welsh Calvinistic Methodist Chapel. The Chapel was a very important part of family life: it was a social centre for the church families. Many years later, after Martyn Lloyd-Jones had died, Bethan wrote of the first time she saw the man who was to be her husband and life partner for well over fifty years:

In the seat in front of me sat a family I had never seen before. A very handsome, somewhat portly man with a beautiful head of greying wavy hair. Beside him sat his wife—smartly dressed and a good deal younger. With them three boys, the youngest next to his mother wore his 'Eton' collar outside his coat. The middle one [Martyn] slight, with straight black hair brushed across his forehead, and the third very like his father. In the after-meeting, their membership transfer papers were read out and they were received into the church, being introduced as the Lloyd-Jones family from Llangeitho … that was our first meeting.[2]

1. Morgan (1973), 537.
2. Lloyd-Jones (1983), 2.

Dating was unknown at that time, at least among the middle and upper middle classes, and courtship in the 1920s in this stratum of society was something which took place at social events such as tennis competitions. Given that the Phillipses had their own court, it is no surprise to learn that Bethan not only loved tennis but was also very good at it. There were often opportunities for her to play at inter-church matches. Martyn Lloyd-Jones, by contrast, hated tennis, but such was his love for Bethan that he attempted it, though with little degree of success. He was only a mediocre player in doubles, less so in singles, and, perhaps not unsurprisingly, given that he was clearly outshone by other admirers of Bethan, directed quite a lot of criticism at the 'craze' for the game. He was only human, after all!

Bethan and Martyn's paths crossed on and off for a period of some nine years. As far as a serious relationship with him was concerned—that is, one which would lead to marriage—Bethan's chief reservation was that she was eighteen months older than he and that he was, therefore, too young.

The cultural norms of the day meant that there would be very little of getting to know someone of the opposite sex in private. Instead, a man would meet a young woman in company with others and, at the appropriate time, would simply propose to her as the woman of his dreams. Martyn Lloyd-Jones had been the first person to ask for Bethan's hand in marriage, but she declined. In addition to their different views on things, which frequently led them to argue, and their different social backgrounds, the age-gap between them mattered to Bethan and this had a significant effect upon her before they became very good friends: she simply could not countenance being older than a 'would-be admirer'. But there were to be many more suitors. All in all, Bethan Phillips received twenty-seven proposals of marriage, as well as being aware of the fact that 'the scion of one titled family was decidedly interested'.[3] Two of her suitors were ministers who 'fell in love' with her while preaching, each of whom wrote to her the next

---

3. Catherwood (1995), 31.

day to declare his undying love! But Bethan was being kept for the most illustrious suitor of them all, who would propose on a second occasion to her. This time she would accept, and Martyn Lloyd-Jones would secure the hand of the woman of his dreams.

What changed her mind?

To begin with, she realised that love is more than skin deep. She began to have second thoughts about this 'very interesting young man' who was in and out of her life. She had to admit just how interested she had become in him when one day she was told by a friend—mistakenly—that he had become engaged to a nurse. Her hand froze on her hair brush when she heard this. Her friend's remark proved to be a jolt to her, helping her to realise that she *was* attracted to him. How often a seemingly insignificant remark or event can prove to be a turning point! It is clear from a letter which Martyn wrote to Bethan's brother Ieuan in February 1925 that the two were becoming very close. By this date, Martyn was very exercised in his spirit about committing himself to the work of gospel ministry. In this connection he had a tremendous burden for his home country of Wales. The following words indicate that romance was indeed blossoming:

> *I thought of you several times this evening while I was with Bethan. I really think that she is now about as determined about Wales as I am—Ieuan, she almost makes a vital difference to me and yet when she asked me the other day whether she or Wales came first, I had to say that Wales came first. That was certainly the most awful question I have yet been asked during my life. She was great enough to say that she thought still more of me for saying that.*[4]

Engagement

'In the Spring a young man's fancy lightly turns to thoughts of love'.[5] On the day after Good Friday 1926, Martyn invited Bethan

---

4. Murray (1994), 6.

5. From Alfred, Lord Tennyson's 'Locksley Hall'.

to accompany him and two friends to Westminster Chapel the following evening to hear Dr John Hutton preach. Bethan readily accepted. On Sunday, learning that she was free the following day—which was a Bank Holiday—he invited her to a picnic in a country park, and again Bethan responded positively. Arguments had already become a thing of the past. Indeed, their major disagreement throughout life was only that of who loved whom the more, which is surely a blessed kind of disagreement to have. By June of the same year, Martyn Lloyd-Jones and Bethan Phillips were engaged to be married. The week before her engagement, Bethan obtained her Bachelor of Surgery. However, the 'church family' were to know their secret before the ring was bought:

> *Parental approval being readily given, Martyn meant no official engagement to be announced until he could purchase a ring on the following Tuesday. But at Charing Cross on Sunday, June 18, Bethan's elation was too much to be explained solely by her University success: before the evening service the secret was out and round the whole chapel.*[6]

Although Martyn came from humbler origins than Bethan—his family being in the dairy business (although there was considerable 'snobbishness' amongst the London Welsh in this line of work)—marriage to an exceptionally gifted physician who, in addition to having a Harley Street practice, was Chief Clinical Assistant to Lord Horder, the King's physician, would have meant that Bethan—in the language of that time—would not have been marrying 'below her station'. Dr Lloyd-Jones had already been a guest at dinner parties at the country estate of Horder, meeting there some of the leading figures of the day. If Bethan had been interested only in wealth and social position, then she had indeed 'made a good match'. But, in the language of today, she had much higher values. By the summer of 1926 when they were engaged, Bethan already

---

6. Murray (1982), 105.

knew that her husband-to-be would not be pursuing the illustrious medical career which had already begun to open up before him. As they discussed their future together she became aware of his overwhelming conviction that he must preach. He had a passion to tell others of Christ. Later she would recall what was animating him at that time:

> ... *how on fire he was to tell people what Christianity meant, and his wish to be in some raw place where people were conscious of their need.*[7]

The words 'a raw place' are significant: for not only would this mean a change for Martyn from the affluent life of a Harley Street physician, but it would also mean that Bethan must leave the comfortable surroundings of her parents' Harrow home, not for some other privileged situation but, with her new husband, for something very different. Wales was still very much on his heart.

Marriage to Martyn also meant that Bethan would be giving up *her* medical career in order fully to support her husband in his new sphere of work. In December 1926, Martyn ended his full-time commitment to medicine, and Bethan was wholeheartedly behind him. She said: 'I was proud to share with him those difficulties which followed his decision to leave medicine'. And share she would through their long years of marriage together.

> *Therefore, I urge you, brothers [and sisters], in view of God's mercy, to offer your bodies as living sacrifices, holy and pleasing to God—this is your spiritual act of worship. Do not conform any longer to the pattern of this world, but be transformed by the renewing of your mind. Then you will be able to test and approve what God's will is—his good, pleasing and perfect will.*
> ROMANS 12:1–2

---

7. ibid., 108.

The Lloyd-Jones family at Regency Street: Henry and Magdalene
Lloyd-Jones, with Harold (front), Martyn (back left) and Vincent.[1]

4

A WIFE FOR ALL SEASONS

Wives, submit to your husbands, as is fitting in the
Lord ... the wife must respect her husband.
COLOSSIANS 3:18; EPHESIANS 5:33

The Puritan ethic of marriage was first to look not for a
partner whom you do love passionately at this moment
but rather for one you can love steadily as your best friend
for life, then proceed with God as help and do just that.
J.I. PACKER

A change of place

In an age when many marriages turned sour, when many strata of
society had 'mistresses', and when some men regarded women as
chattels, it is wonderful to see the care and love which the Lloyd-
Joneses had one for another. Although Bethan never failed to share
her husband with all God's people, they always made time for one
another: their marriage beams out pure and bright and still speaks
today into a nation which is being destroyed by infidelity and a
lack of commitment.

Bethan Phillips and Martyn Lloyd-Jones were married on 8 January, 1927 at Charing Cross Chapel. (It is interesting to note that

the great Charles Haddon Spurgeon was married on the same date in 1856.) The *South Wales News* reported:

> *It will be remembered that Dr Martyn Lloyd-Jones recently created a sensation by announcing his intention to relinquish his practice in Harley Street for the pulpit, and he has now accepted an invitation to become lay-pastor of Bethlehem Forward Movement Mission Hall, Sandfields, Aberavon. His bride, Dr Bethan Phillips, is also giving up her medical work at the University College Hospital to help her husband in his religious duties at Aberavon. The bride, who was given away by her father, was attired in a gown of white charmeuse and lace. Her bridal veil was of tulle surmounted with a wreath of orange blossom; and she carried a bouquet of white roses.*[1]

They had a short honeymoon, and intended to move immediately after this to their new sphere of work at Aberavon. They had to postpone the move, however, because they had unfinished business in London. Even with this change in plans they still fully intended to arrive in South Wales by 26 January. But it was not to be: Martyn came down with influenza and was unable to go anywhere. Consequently, they had to delay their move to South Wales until he recovered.

Therefore, it was not until the beginning of February that they eventually left London and arrived at Aberavon, which was part of Port Talbot, the scene of her husband's first pastorate. It was an immense change for this young couple—especially for Bethan: London to Aberavon; a large home with tennis court and servants to a small terraced house, which has been described as follows:

> *… a parlour or best room at the front, a 'middle room' behind it (with French window opening on to a small yard), and a living room and scullery-kitchen occupying the narrow oblong extremity of the house which lay furthest back from the front*

1. Murray (1982), 126.

*door. Up a staircase near the front-door there were three
bedrooms and, in the eyes of some visitors, an amazingly small
bathroom. The front of the house was almost immediately on
the street and behind there was a small garden.*[2]

But Mrs Lloyd-Jones rose to the challenge. For the first week, they
had to lodge with a family from the church—the Robsons—while
the decorating of the manse was completed. This must have been
quite a strain for a newly married couple, moving into a home with
people they hardly knew. Bethan said years later: 'I look back with
a grateful heart for all the help that Mrs Robson gave to me—she
was truly a "mother in Israel"'. Violet Robson was an example of
'another godly woman'.[3] Marjorie, Mrs Robson's daughter, says she
remembers how easy the Lloyd-Joneses were to have in the home.
They liked things plain and simple: toast and tea-cake for tea. One
can well imagine that if this had not been their custom, it soon
would have become their practice in order to make life as easy as
possible for the Robson household, who had kindly opened their
home to them.

The first night there, however, nearly proved to be their last.
The bedroom in which Martyn and Bethan slept had a gas lamp
connected to the wall. The last task of the evening was for Mr
Robson to allow the family to prepare for bed before he turned the
gas off at the mains. The Lloyd-Joneses, unused to gas lamps, and
probably taking longer than the family to retire for bed, did not turn
their gas lamp off when the light went out. As a result, therefore,
early the next morning when Mr Robson turned the mains supply
back on, gas came billowing into their room. Fortunately, Bethan
woke up and was able to throw open a window and raise the alarm.
What a mercy for them—and for the church—that she woke at
that very moment! These two lives, whom God was going to use

2. ibid., 153.

3. See Appendix 2.

mightily, could have been brought to an untimely end. But the Lord had much for them to do.

In everything Bethan did as she adjusted to her new life, she sought to identify with the people amongst whom God had set her. Marjorie remembers her mother saying how thoughtful Mrs Lloyd-Jones had been when she came to Aberavon. The many expensive wedding gifts which they had received from friends in London were carefully stored away. Although Bethan had been used to quite a luxurious lifestyle, the Lloyd-Jones' home was furnished very modestly.

Bethan wanted everyone who called to feel at home and welcome. She never wanted people to feel that somehow she and Martyn were 'above' the rest. This was also the case when it came to the way she dressed. She wanted to fit into the place to which God had called them. Marjorie Robson recalled the first time she saw Mrs Lloyd-Jones: 'She was dressed so simply and looked so pretty'. To dress in any other way other than 'simply' would have drawn a great deal of unhelpful attention to Bethan, and, given the considerable poverty of the area, it would have done little to settle and commend her and her husband to the folk amongst whom they had come to live. 'Caesar's wife must be above reproach'. Years later, Mrs Lloyd-Jones commented on the social deprivation which characterised the town:

> *At that time Aberavon was beginning to suffer from the great depression ... There were bunches of lads on the street corners who had left school four or five years before, and had never had a day's work since. A general air of depression overspread the district.*[4]

This was, of course, in stark contrast to the surroundings in which she had lived and grown up. Her early days in Aberavon presented her, therefore, with numerous challenges, all at the same time: her

---

4. Lloyd-Jones (1983), 3.

new surroundings, her new marital status, and the change from a Welsh to an English-speaking church. A lesser but just as real challenge was in the kitchen! Today, there are cookery programmes galore on the television to encourage human beings of every conceivable kind—whether young unmarried or 'unattached' men who share a house, upwardly mobile, single young women, or young couples who work from early morning till late into the evening—to forgo fast foods and ready meals and to explore their hidden culinary abilities. One may be tempted to think that it was not always so: if not the men, surely women in the past knew their way around the kitchen. However, this was certainly not always the case. After the Lloyd-Joneses had moved into their new home in Aberavon, it was Mrs Robson who cooked their first chicken meal for them, for the simple reason that at the beginning of her married life Bethan was completely undomesticated. She had, of course, been used to having the services of a cook when she lived at home with her parents. Mrs Robson was a kindly lady with a big heart, and she took something of a motherly interest in this young minister's wife: cooking Bethan's first chicken meal for the young couple was a very practical demonstration of Christian love. She helped in other ways too. Quite often Dr Lloyd-Jones would invite people back for a cup of tea and forget to tell his wife. Mrs Robson and another member of the church, Mrs McDonald, lived just a few doors away, so it was easy for Bethan to send to them for things like cake if she had unexpected visitors. They were good neighbours to have, and often stepped into the breach. There were frequent visitors to the home: many came from far and wide to see 'the Doctor' for medical as well as spiritual advice. The home at Aberavon was always open, so Bethan quickly learned to adapt to this new role.

An anxious heart

Although Bethan Lloyd-Jones was in many ways an accomplished young lady and blessed with a strong personality she was, nevertheless, of a very anxious disposition. She was terrified when she heard gales blowing in from the sea, remembering how the first two Aberavons had come to their end, having been swept away by the force of the waves. She said, 'I had even bought a timetable of the tides, so that I would know the times of the high tides, especially when the moon was at the full!'[5] One cannot help wondering if knowledge of when there would be high tides would have increased, rather than have helped, her anxiety! She evidently suffered at this time from high anxiety or, as one of her grandchildren put it, 'a very developed imagination'. Bethan recalled:

> One night when Martyn was away, and I was alone with the baby, there was an exceptionally severe gale blowing in from the sea and I lay, beside myself with fear, tossing feverishly in bed, full of terror and panic—if the tide came up Victoria Road, could I escape with the baby? Get out of the window? On to the roof etc. At last, in sheer helpless despair, I got out of my bed and on to my knees, and prayed: 'Lord, if it is all true, if you are really there and will answer my prayer, please give me peace and take all my fear away'. As I spoke, it all went away, my heart was flooded with perfect peace, and I never had any more fear of floods and tides. I was completely delivered and asleep in two minutes. As the hymn says: 'The Lord is rich and merciful, the Lord is very kind.'[6]

She felt she could not have gone on much longer in Aberavon without such a deliverance. The fact of the matter was that, although she had been so fearful of the house being swept away, it was something about which she had not confided in her husband. Possibly she was concerned that this might have curtailed him in his work as he travelled away to preach. Had he been aware of the problem, no doubt he would have given her the kind of pastoral counsel which he was to give to so many to help them overcome their fears. In this case,

---

5. Murray (1982), 239

6. ibid.

however, deliverance came directly from the Lord, and a valuable lesson was learned concerning the life of prayer. But vital though this lesson was, there was something even greater which Bethan needed to learn, and in this matter her husband *did* play a part.

A change of heart

Dr Lloyd-Jones' ministry was wonderfully used by God to bring all kinds of people to salvation: not only to those who were outwardly and obviously in great need, but also to those who were religious. And Bethan Lloyd-Jones was one such person who needed to be brought to salvation. Something of her awareness that all was not right between her and God may be seen in the way in which she viewed the conversion of some of the town's less reputable characters and compared this with her own experience:

> *I was born into a Christian family, 'christened' as a baby, confirming the christening on becoming a church member at 12 years old, and so I did not know what else was needed. I was afraid of God, and afraid of dying, and eschewed evil because of this. I tried to do all a 'Christian' should do in such duties as church attendance and I accepted the Bible as the Word of God. But I had no inner peace or joy and I knew nothing of the glorious release of the gospel …*
>
> *I rejoiced to see men and women converted … and I envied them and sometimes wished, when I saw their radiant faces and changed lives, that I had been a drunkard or worse, so that I could be converted! I never imagined that I needed to be converted, having always been a 'Christian' or that I could get any more than I had already! … God graciously used Martyn's morning sermons to open my eyes and show me myself and my need.*[7]

---

7. Lloyd-Jones (1983), 5.

But it was not only her husband's preaching which made a deep impression upon her. On one occasion, a notable character who was a member of the Sandfields church was on the same bus as Bethan and asked her, in his characteristically blunt way, 'Now Mrs Jones, your husband is always saying we must be born again. Well, how about you Mrs Jones, are you saved?' The question had a profound effect upon her. Having attended church and prayer meetings from childhood, she had always believed herself to be a Christian. But now, she was becoming aware of her need of personal salvation.

It was when Bethan heard Martyn preach for the first time, on his second visit to Sandfields in December 1926, that she was confronted with the reality of her situation. Dr Lloyd-Jones underlined the fact that all people were equally in need of salvation from sin. The message shook her, even frightened her. Although she had always, in a sense, feared God and had sought to live an upright life, she had no personal assurance of the forgiveness of sins. Common grace had certainly been at work in her life. She had so many of the outward characteristics of a Christian, without being truly converted. She had a certain 'natural' goodness, but no real understanding of the gospel. Years later she explained her situation at this time:

> I was two years under Martyn's ministry before I really understood what the gospel was. I used to listen to him on a Sunday morning and I used to feel, 'Well, if this is Christianity I don't really know anything about it....' I recall sitting in the study at Victoria Road and I was unhappy. I suppose it was conviction. I felt a burden of sin, and I shall always remember Martyn saying, as he looked through his books, 'Read John Angell James—"The Anxious Enquirer Directed"'. I have never forgotten what I read in that book. It showed me how wrong was the idea that my sin could be greater than the merit

*of the blood of Christ—his death was well able to clear all my
sins away. There, at last, I found release and I was happy.*[8]

We may well ask how it was that Dr Lloyd-Jones ever married
someone who was unconverted, but to answer that question, we
need to understand something of the times in which they were
living, as well as the background and context of Mrs Lloyd-Jones'
upbringing. The Doctor himself had not long been in possession
of 'heart religion'. Chapel attendance was the order of the day, and
there was a widespread assumption on the part of many in the
chapels that chapel attendance and seeking to live a good life were
what constituted true Christianity. Could it be that the Doctor
regarded Bethan at the time of their marriage as being a truly
converted woman? Certainly she came from an evangelical family
that believed in the importance of new birth, and the 'goodness'
of her character might easily have been mistaken for genuine
Christian holiness. It was only under her husband's searching
ministry that she realised that she was a stranger to salvation. Or
might it be that at this stage in his Christian experience the Doctor
had not grasped the importance of marrying only 'in the Lord'? We
shall probably never know the answers to these questions. What
we do know is that in response to Martyn, many, like Bethan, were
experiencing new life in Christ:

> *There were confessions of faith, conversions and requests for
> membership throughout the Aberavon ministry—not always
> in large numbers, but usually one or two in the after meeting
> on most Sundays. We always sang the doxology after their
> reception by the minister and there were not many Sundays
> when the doxology was not sung.*[9]

Dr Lloyd-Jones had a happy and fruitful ministry in this South
Wales town, fully supported by his wife in his work, during the

8. Murray (1982), 166–67.

9. ibid., 287 (footnote).

eleven and a half years that they were there. Although the Doctor had had numerous invitations from other churches to become their pastor, he had felt no inclination to leave the people he loved and served. It was, therefore, a huge wrench for Mrs Lloyd-Jones, as well as for her husband, when they left their spiritual family at Sandfields at the end of July 1938. Bethan later recalled:

> *The memory of the Sunday-night after-meeting, at which the Minister told the congregation that the end of July would mark the conclusion of his ministry with them, is still etched indelibly on my mind. At that time it seemed unreal; I could not believe what I was hearing. And yet the call to Martyn was clear and unmistakable ... as he himself described it, it was as though 'a shutter had come down' and he knew that the time had come to leave his first charge. Leaving Sandfields was certainly not easy ... we did not see everything clearly, but were walking by faith.*[10]

The war years

On leaving Aberavon in 1938 the Lloyd-Jones family—Dr and Mrs Lloyd-Jones, and their two daughters, Elizabeth and Ann—were to have a holiday at Talybont, Cardiganshire, after which they were to stay with Martyn's mother in London for a number of months while they waited to discern the Lord's will with respect to their future. Both believed that God was sovereign and would overrule for their good in the way He would lead them—and they waited! When it became clear that they would not be moving back to Wales—there had been a possibility of the Doctor becoming Principal of the Calvinistic Methodist College in Bala—but would be remaining in London, they decided to buy a house. The Doctor began ministering at Westminster Chapel for some months alongside Dr Campbell Morgan, and the following year he became associate minister at the Chapel. However, the Lloyd-Joneses were unable to

---

10. Lloyd-Jones (1983), 103.

complete their house purchase because of the outbreak of war, and this prevented them as a family from settling down in London. In late August 1939 Martyn, Bethan and their family were in Llanelli, South Wales, where the Doctor had a preaching engagement. A Mr and Mrs Pearce, who lived in Llanelli, offered to accommodate Mrs Lloyd-Jones and the children in a separate wing of their large family home, as the outbreak of World War II was then imminent. This meant that Martyn travelled back to London on his own, and thus began a period of separation for the whole family.

Mrs Lloyd-Jones was, quite obviously, very anxious about her husband being in London: she felt that while she and the girls were in the comparative safety of the countryside, her husband was living in constant danger of being bombed. Evidence of this anxiety can be seen in the way that Martyn sought, in one of his letters, to reassure her:

Well, Bethan dear, keep your spirit at peace. Leave yourself and me too, and everything in God's hand and you will find peace and rest. You know what it is to do this in other connections. Do the same now.[11]

The Doctor's regular mid-week as well as weekend ministry made it difficult for him to get away from London to be with his family, and thus Bethan saw very little of Martyn during the first few months of the war. It is interesting to note that when Mrs Lloyd-Jones was living in Llanelli during this time, her husband's greatest concern for her, in addition to his concern that she would not become over-tired, was that she should use her mind. He was vexed that she did not have time to read. Another great concern of his was their financial situation: the effect of the war on the congregation at Westminster Chapel was such that the offerings in the church were considerably reduced, and this led the Doctor to accept a reduction in his stipend. He was concerned that Bethan might suffer because

---

11. Murray (1994), 41.

of the essential economies that had to be made: he was concerned for his wife, telling her not to work too hard and to make sure that she was in bed early. His letters always ended with expressions of his love for her and the children, but especially for her as, 'the dearest girl in all the world'. The following extract from one of his letters to her expresses his concerns at this time:

> *There is no need for you to cut back on expense at all. Take care to prepare and to eat proper meals ... Don't worry about the cost of Elizabeth's books ... she has got to have them. I have no faith in you in this matter—none at all—and it is a very real worry to me.*[12]

Those who only knew the Doctor as the minister of a large London church and as a world-famous preacher might well have been ignorant of the struggles which he and Mrs Lloyd-Jones went through during the war. Because of these experiences, they would later be able to identify with fellow believers in difficult situations and be able to give the kind of help which can only be given by those who have had experience of God's help in difficulties (2 Cor.1:3–4).

With their plans of purchasing a house having been put on hold because of the war the Lloyd-Joneses decided to rent a house outside of London, and so it was in December of 1939 that they rented a semi-detached house in Haslemere, Surrey, called 'The Haven'. They would remain there until November 1943. The week before they moved to their new home, Martyn was preaching near Llanelli and arranged to meet Bethan in Cardiff. His concern for her comes out in the detailed instructions he wrote her about how and where they would meet:

> *Now, about tomorrow. Here are the 'instructions': You'll arrive probably on Platform 2. If you find, on asking!—that the train is not yet in, walk down the steps to the subway and walk up the steps to Platform 3—the one on which I shall*

12. ibid., 45.

arrive. If you are told that the train is going to be late, go and sit by the fire in the waiting-room. When the train arrives stand on the platform, between the two stairs that lead to the subway. I shall make for that point. If I am in first, I shall stand between the two stairways leading to the subway, on Platform 2. So, have a look there first. We cannot miss each other—if you were in a haystack I'd find you. My only anxiety is that someone else will be trying to get hold of you too! Remember that Cardiff is a very cold place. Put plenty of warm clothes on and eat plenty of breakfast. How to wait for tomorrow I don't know? Till then all my love to you my dear love, and to the two girls.[13]

Although based at Haslemere from the end of 1939, the couple still had to endure periodic times of separation. In the early summer of 1941, for instance, as a result of Bethan needing to rest after having pneumonia, she travelled with her younger daughter, Ann, to her parents, who were now in Newcastle Emlyn and who would look after Ann for her while she convalesced. Martyn and Elizabeth remained in Haslemere. Although this was a necessary parting, for most of the war they were able to be together as a family. One 'enforced' parting during the war years had a humourous aspect to it. Doctor Lloyd-Jones had to go north to preach for the best part of a week. There was a very real threat of bombs falling in London, and although the Lloyd-Joneses were living some distance from the capital city, the Doctor was aware that Mrs Lloyd-Jones was fearful. He arranged, therefore, for his wife and children to stay with a friend who was a farmer—a Mr Rodwell—and his family at Harston in the Cambridgeshire countryside. While they were there, two bombs exploded in adjacent fields! Ann was seven at the time and heard the noise of the approaching 'flying' bomb. She always seemed to be aware of their presence. Ann simply said: 'Oh, one of them!' They flung themselves to the floor as the bomb headed

13. Murray (1990), 41–42.

away from them—and exploded just two fields away. So much for safety in the country!

The Doctor needed to travel from Surrey to London each Saturday night to ensure that he was there to preach on Sunday. However, since the railways were operating to war time schedules, he could never be certain that he would arrive when expected. This being the case, it was far too difficult for Bethan and the girls to accompany him, and so it was decided that throughout this period—which was to stretch from December 1939 until November 1943, after which the family would move back to London—they should attend a local Congregational church. So, for the best part of four years, the Doctor did not have his wife with him in the church of which he was the minister. Had Bethan Lloyd-Jones been the sort of woman who craved to be the centre of attention as a minister's wife or who saw herself as somehow involved in 'running the church', these would have been extraordinarily difficult years for her. But, like Susannah Spurgeon, she saw herself as one who was to glorify God by 'giving up her lamb' to the Lord, and this she certainly did during this time.

As we have seen, for the Lloyd-Joneses, any period of separation was more a case of 'absence makes the heart grow fonder' than 'out of sight, out of mind'. If he was away from her for more than forty-eight hours, the Doctor would telephone his wife each night—no mobile or smart phones in those days!—and also send a letter. The devotion between them was very evident in these little tokens of his love for her. Weary of the constant commuting back and forth to London, and given that the heavy bombing over the city had ceased towards the end of 1943—at least, for the time being—the family decided to move from Haslemere back to London. A new home was found for them in Colebrook Avenue, Ealing, and they moved there in November 1943. Much of their furniture, which had been stored in Cardiff, was now transported to London. However, they stayed less than two years at this property because at the end of this period the owners wanted to sell the house. The asking price was £2,500, which was more than the Lloyd-Joneses could afford. So it was that in July 1945 they moved to 39 Mount Park Crescent, Ealing: a roomy, three-storeyed, Edwardian house, and here they would remain longer than in any other place in which they had lived—or would live.

Coping with criticism

If Bethan could be impartial and objective in her constructive criticism of her husband, it was no less the case that she was able to maintain a right and proper detachment when others were unfair and destructive in their criticism of the Doctor. Their early years at Westminster were, in this respect, far from easy, especially coming after eleven years in the very supportive and loving atmosphere of the church at Sandfields. In the years when Dr Lloyd-Jones shared the ministry with Dr Campbell Morgan as associate pastor, there were influential members and deacons who quite openly expressed their preference for the latter's ministry, and one prominent member would not even attend when Bethan's husband was preaching. After Campbell Morgan's retirement in 1943 it seems that there were deacons who manoeuvered to get the Doctor to leave the Chapel. Mrs Lloyd-Jones must have felt for her husband in all this and, therefore, must have seen how unfair and unjust it was. However, while supportive of her husband, she did not publicly 'rush to his defence'. She wrote:

> *Of course there were those who did not want him, he was far too evangelical for them—he even made them 'feel like sinners'! I know I just watched and waited, and saw how, in nearly every case, he—or his gospel—won them and many who had been less than inviting became his firmest friends.*[14]

Possibly one of the most testing and trying incidents in the whole of Dr Lloyd-Jones' ministry was the public disagreement between him and John Stott at the Opening Rally of the National Assembly

---

14. Murray (1990), 101.

of Evangelicals at Westminster Central Hall, London, in October 1966. The Doctor had been invited, by a Commission on Church Unity which had been set up by the Evangelical Alliance, to state in public before the Assembly the views which he held on church unity and which he had already shared privately with the Commission. The chairman for the evening was the Revd John Stott, the Rector of All Souls, Langham Place the largest evangelical Anglican church in London at that time. It would not be an overstatement to say that Dr Lloyd-Jones and John Stott were the two most influential evangelical preachers in London at that time and, indeed, in England and Wales, and probably in the UK at large. Moreover, they were both influential within the then IVF (now UCCF, the evangelical body which works amongst students) and had spoken together at conferences. When, therefore, at the close of Dr Lloyd-Jones' address to the meeting, John Stott took the unusual—not to say unprecedented—step of publicly disagreeing with him (saying that both Scripture and history were against what the Doctor had said), it created something of a sensation and it was inevitable that something of a polarisation would occur between evangelicals within the UK—some adopting the Doctor's position while others followed that of John Stott.

Much has already been written about this, and I refer my readers to what others, who are more qualified to comment upon this, have said upon the issue. Suffice it to say, as the official biographers of both men have been at pains to point out, there was absolutely nothing of a personal nature in the disagreement, and neither of the men can be blamed for some of the intemperate remarks which have been made and the bitter attitudes which have been displayed by some believers on both sides of this matter. To John Stott's great credit, he later apologised to the Doctor for the place and timing of his remarks—but not for what he had said; similarly, it was the Doctor's great desire that the public breach be healed and that the two men be visibly together. In it all, however, the effect upon Mrs Lloyd-Jones can—and has been—easily and largely overlooked. Even her own brother Ieuan—Dr Lloyd-Jones' best friend—thought very differently on these issues. Although the Doctor had encouraged men to leave denominations which contained both evangelicals and non-evangelicals in order to come together in a loose fellowship of evangelical churches, his brother-in-law remained in the Presbyterian Church of Wales. Such things can often cause a real strain within a family and amongst friends. However, Bethan never allowed her husband's, or her own beliefs and principles, to affect or spoil fellowship with her brother or any other Christian. Right up to Ieuan's death they all remained the best of friends. It is interesting to note that this love for all the brethren persisted throughout Mrs Lloyd-Jones' life. (It should also be noted that the Doctor maintained close *personal* friendship and fellowship with those who did not follow his lead on this matter. He was a *big* man: while he would not compromise on *principles*, he was mindful that *people* matter as well as principles. Sadly, not all who adopted his principles on issues of church separation and unity adopted this large-heartedness with respect to brothers who may not have seen things as he did.)

John Stott was a bachelor, and therefore his part in the controversy affected only him: he had no wife who might have felt for him in this very public disagreement. But how did Mrs Lloyd-Jones cope with what was clearly one of the most public criticisms ever made of her husband, and that not from those who were opposed to the gospel, but from a fellow gospel minister? It would have been all too easy for her to have become bitter towards the younger man. Yet an incident which occurred two years later and which has thus far not been reported shows just how far she was from holding a grudge or nurturing bitterness.

In 1968, Dr Lloyd-Jones had to undergo major emergency surgery to remove a blockage caused by cancer. At this time Mrs Lloyd-Jones was with her daughter Ann one evening at the hospital. Ann remembers John Stott coming to the hospital and, with tears in his eyes, asking her mother if he was responsible for causing the cancer. He was obviously referring to the public disagreement two years earlier, the 'fall out' this had occasioned within the evangelical community in this country, and the inevitable strain which this must have placed upon the Doctor. Moreover, the question was being posed to Mrs Lloyd-Jones at a time of considerable stress. How easy it would have been for her to have ignored the younger man! (Alas! One has heard of Christians behaving like this in situations which are far less fraught.) How tempting it must have been to have made an unkind comment! But 'love is kind … it is not easily angered, it keeps no record of wrongs' (1 Cor. 13:4–5). She simply and affectionately put her hand on his arm and told him not to be so silly and foolish. She beckoned to a nurse and asked if she and John Stott could have the use of a room for some moments. Mrs Lloyd-Jones took this initiative so they could spend some time in prayer before she suggested to Stott that he go in to see the Doctor, which he did. Like her husband, she was well able to distinguish between personality and principles, and the law of kindness was on her lips. What an example of true Christian love and concern!

Constant love

Bethan's greatest labour of love was keeping her husband in the pulpit. How did she do this? First and foremost, she offered him up to God and His service. Maybe those of us who are ministers' wives will need to remember this at times when we have to share our husbands with so many people. It is only with and by God's grace that we can give up our 'lamb' as Bethan so graciously did. Someone once asked her how she could constantly part with her husband and share him with so many. She simply replied, 'I regard it the greatest privilege of my life to be married to such a godly man.' She made no reference to her own privation. The important principle here was that Mrs Lloyd-Jones was willing to give him up to God, just as many others before her had done with their husbands. Because she was so often in the background, few realised just how dependent her husband was upon her.

Bethan was her husband's best critic—as Ann Phillips had been with Bethan's grandfather. Mrs Lloyd-Jones was not afraid to make her views known: if she felt he had been a bit too long in his delivery of a sermon, she would tell him, and would also make any other comment which she felt would be helpful and profitable to him. Dr Lloyd-Jones once said, jokingly, that the only time he felt like filing for a divorce was when Mrs Lloyd-Jones had passed her 'verdict' on one of his sermons![15] In reality, of course, she was—as he wrote in the preface to his *Studies in the Sermon on the Mount*—'my best and severest critic'. She never stood in such awe of him that she feared to express her opinions. It was a very happy marriage, in which neither party was slave to the other. Each would weigh what the other said and would accept the criticism if it was fair. This, of course, is an aspect of that true, heavenly wisdom which is submissive or, as the Authorised Version renders it, 'easy to be entreated'. Bethan would never nag her husband, but if she felt a course of action was not right, she would simply say, 'You know what I believe, but we'll leave it at that.' After such an exchange, and after some consideration, the Doctor would often end up choosing what she had suggested. Bethan was always such an unselfish woman and, therefore, an unselfish wife: she was more concerned for her husband's welfare than for her own. This can be seen in a letter which she wrote to some friends:

---

15. This information came to me from my husband, who heard it from the late Graham Harrison. Mr Harrison was a Welsh minister who was close to Dr Lloyd-Jones' theological outlook on a range of issues: the 'primacy of preaching'; his views of the work of the Holy Spirit and of revival; and his doctrine of the church. Mr Harrison took part in the Doctor's funeral. He was a regular attender at the Westminster Fellowship of ministers, which met in Westminster Chapel each month, and attended the Minister's Conference of The Evangelical Movement of Wales held in Bala each year, at which the Doctor chaired the evening discussion sessions and at which he gave the closing address. My husband's recollection is that the Doctor made this remark, jokingly, at one of these events.

This is an excellent place for Martyn to have a rest (almost as good as Bryn Uchaf!). He was very tired after such a hard season—preaching and travelling non-stop throughout the country, and he is looking forward to starting again in the New Year, God willing. Through God's grace he is enjoying good health and in his element with all the work.[16]

The letter makes no reference to her own needs: her joy was to do all that she could to serve and help him in his great work for the gospel. She once said to a minister's wife:

'Now my dear, you must not let your husband work too hard.' 'How do you manage that?' the minister's wife asked, at which Mrs Lloyd-Jones smiled and replied, 'My dear I really don't know!'[17]

There was such a mutual love between husband and wife that they regularly teased one another about it. Testimony to the fact that Martyn loved Bethan very deeply is seen in every letter he ever wrote her. The following extract from a letter which he sent her while she was staying at Llanelli in the early part of the Second World War clearly demonstrates this:

When I think of those days in London 1925–1926, when we thought at the time that it was impossible to love each other more, I feel like laughing. Truly during the last year I have come to believe that a man could not love his wife more than I love you, yet I see there's no end/limit to love, and it is true that 'absence makes the heart grow fonder' I am perfectly sure that there is no lover anywhere who writes to a girl with whom

16. Lloyd-Jones Archive: Lloyd-Jones. (Written in Welsh) No date. Letters deposited in the Lloyd-Jones Archive at The National Library of Wales, Aberystwyth. Hereafter reference to these letters—as distinct from the published letters of Dr Lloyd-Jones—will be identified as: Lloyd-Jones Archive followed by the name of the writer and recipient, if so stated.

17. Catherwood (1986), 234.

he is so 'crazy/infatuated' with [sic], as I am. Indeed I pity those lovers who are not married.[18]

He always wrote to her during his many absences from her when he was travelling around the country preaching, and there are frequent expressions of his great love for her. Martyn, absent without mail for a week, was able to write: 'I do not feel for a moment that you have forgotten me.'

There were times when faithfulness to the truth rendered Martyn Lloyd-Jones one of the loneliest men in the world: this has invariably been the lot of men who have had something of a 'prophetic' dimension to their ministry. Spurgeon referred to the loneliness of the man of God who sees issues with a clarity that sets him apart from many of his contemporaries. Just as Spurgeon's wife was such a great support and source of comfort to him, so it was that, in his wife Bethan, the Doctor had one who was a great encourager and quiet strength to spur him on in the tireless work of preaching the glorious gospel of Christ. What an immeasurably important task she was given, and what true love they shared over so many decades!

Love is patient, love is kind…. Love does not delight in evil but rejoices with the truth. It always protects, always trusts, always hopes, always perseveres. Love never fails … And now these three remain: faith, hope and love. But the greatest of these is love.
1 CORINTHIANS 13:4, 6–8, 13

---

18. Lloyd-Jones Archive: Dr Lloyd-Jones to Mrs Lloyd-Jones.

Martyn and Bethan on their wedding day, 8 January 1927,
Charing Cross Chapel, London.[1]

Bethlehem Forward Movement Hall,
popularly known as Sandfields.1

Bethan with Martyn and Elizabeth on the beach at
Cwm yr Eglwys, Pembrokeshire c.1934.[1]

39 Mount Park Crescent, Ealing. The family home from 1945-65.[2]

5

'CINDERELLA'S CHARIOT FOR ME'

Her children arise and call her blessed …
PROVERBS 31:28

Let your children be as so many flowers, borrowed from God. If the
flowers die or wither, thank God for a summer loan of them.
SAMUEL RUTHERFORD

The ordination baby

Within the first year of the Lloyd-Jones' marriage Elizabeth had
been delivered prematurely, on 26 October 1927. I say 'delivered'
because it had been discovered that there could be complications in
the birth; and so, taking the advice of a Swansea specialist, Bethan
had returned to her parents' home in London during September.
The next month, Elizabeth was delivered by Caesarean-section. The
day of her husband's ordination service at Whitefield's Tabernacle
on Tottenham Court Road was, to say the least, not to be without its
anxieties and pressures. Although the baby had been safely delivered
in the morning, Bethan had haemorrhaged severely and was quite
unwell, and this caused considerable anxiety to her family.

One consequence of Martyn's concern for his wife's health
was that, before the ordination sermon had been preached, the

Doctor left the service in order to be at Bethan's side at the hospital. There were many unique features to Dr Lloyd-Jones' ministry: not being present to hear the sermon preached at his own ordination is probably one of them! Had Mrs Lloyd-Jones not survived, how different things would have been for her husband and, no doubt, for his ministry. But the Lord's purposes were otherwise and, mercifully, she survived. But nine years later, before the birth of her second child, she feared that she would not survive. Shortly before Ann was born in 1937 Bethan had convinced herself—not on the basis of any medical evidence, be it said—that she would die in childbirth. Given the complications she had experienced and the trauma connected with the delivery of her first child it is hardly surprising that she may have felt very anxious. However, she was so certain that she would not see her family again after the birth of her second child that she arranged to have a photograph taken for her family. Happily, her fears proved to be ungrounded: Ann was safely delivered, and the family circle was now complete. Interestingly, Elizabeth believes this photograph to be the most beautiful one which they, as a family, have of their mother.

Care in the home

In most middle class families at that time, the home was never without a maid. Bethan, of course, had grown up in a home where there had always been help with household chores, and after she married Dr Lloyd-Jones and went to live in Aberavon they had a Welsh maid named Belyn. She was eighteen years old when she came to them and remained with the family for ten years. Elizabeth was particularly fond of her. Belyn was followed by Theresa, who went to London with them and remained in service to them for some time. However, when Bethan was staying in Llanelli during the war, she had no paid help there, and, in addition to looking after her daughters, she had all the cooking, cleaning, and washing to do—no automatic washing machines in those days!—while her husband was living in London preaching and overseeing the work of the church.

For someone like Bethan, who was not by nature domesticated and who had been brought up in a comfortable, upper middle class family, now to be without even a maid was a considerable adjustment to her circumstances. This possibly explains why the Doctor was concerned that she would not have time to use her mind. However, she was nothing if not adaptable and a woman who was possessed of the 'rare jewel of Christian contentment', and her extra workload never worried her as she gave herself fully to each task. War usually changes many things in a society; after the war ended, apart from a brief period later in the 1950s, the pattern of functioning without a maid continued in the Lloyd-Jones' household.

Her willingness to adapt does not mean, however, that Bethan had equal enjoyment in all that she did. Those wives who find cooking to be more of a chore than a pleasure might take heart from the fact that cooking was something which she never really enjoyed— although she became quite a good cook. Cleaning, on the other hand, was something which she undertook with great relish. A widowed minister once forbade his wife-to-be to enter his study because, he said, 'There's enough dust in there to make another man!' This was emphatically *not* the case in the Lloyd-Jones' household as long as Bethan was alive. It was as if dust particles went into retreat at the sight of her! Who was it who said that cleanliness is next to godliness? Certainly tidiness and order help in the functioning of a home.

Quite a number of years after moving back to London, in January 1957, the Lloyd-Joneses employed a French maid named Marinette. (Around this time, maids began to be called 'au pairs'.) Bethan wrote to a friend:

You will be interested to hear, that—for the time being at least—we have a <u>maid</u>! She is the sister of Elizabeth's maid, Marinette, aged 21, and a very good girl she is too. I am delighted to have her and though she has only been here a week (tomorrow) she has made a great difference to me already and I feel quite a load lifted off me. She sleeps with

her sister in Elizabeth's house & comes here in the day. It's
something we haven't had for the last 17½ years & I find it
quite a problem to accommodate myself to this strange new
routine, but I find it quite wonderful that every task is no
longer sitting there waiting for me to do it![1]

Once her room was decorated and ready, Marinette went to live
with the Lloyd-Joneses. Bethan and Marinette got on well together
and had a very easy relationship. Before long, the maid had taken
over the running of the home. She would *inform* Mrs Lloyd-Jones:
'I shall be doing the bedrooms this morning so you *won't* be able
to go into them for an hour or so!' She was a good maid and much
loved by the family, but was very much in charge. In fact, she
became like another sister to Ann, and was converted under Dr
Lloyd-Jones' ministry. Marinette would often accompany them to
Llanymawddwy, the home of Mari and John Jones in North Wales,
who were very good friends of the Lloyd-Joneses. It was while on
one of these visits with Bethan that Marinette met a Christian
farmer with whom she would fall in love and marry. Consequently,
she remained in North Wales. (One more maid was to follow, Dina,
before there were no more maids.) Marinette kept in touch with Dr
and Mrs Lloyd-Jones and, on the death of Bethan's brother, Ieuan,
sent the following letter on February 12, 1969:

Dear Mrs Lloyd-Jones,
It is with very great sadness that I heard of your brother's death
and we do send you and your family our sincere condolence.
He was such a kind and humble man and he will be missed
terribly by all his family and all who knew him.

Please be assured of our greatest sympathy in these sad
moments.
                    With our love, Marinette.[2]

---

1. Lloyd-Jones Archive: Bethan Lloyd-Jones to a friend. January 1957.

2. Lloyd-Jones Archive: Marinette to Mrs Lloyd-Jones. February 1969.

Care for her children

Dr and Mrs Lloyd-Jones were devoted to their daughters, both of whom would say that they had wonderful parents: the heavy demands which the Doctor's public ministry placed upon him never made him 'distant' from his children or caused them to feel at a disadvantage. It is interesting to note, however, that although both parents were equally solicitous of their children's welfare, it was Mrs Lloyd-Jones who displayed a greater measure of impartiality with respect to her daughters if anything had upset them. At such times she would ask, 'Are you sure you didn't do anything to provoke things?' In such situations it was she who was objective, whereas the Doctor would instinctively be more protective of his daughters. (So much for the stereotype that men are rational and governed by reason, while women are governed by their emotions! Might it rather be the stereotype of a father taking the side of his daughters?!) Ann certainly believes that her mother was more even handed and objective in this area, which, she says, was good for her because it made her think. Her mother would say, 'Don't tell your father if anyone says anything to hurt you.' She knew he would be as upset as the children themselves!

Mrs Lloyd-Jones was an 'immediate' disciplinarian: her handling of the misdemeanor came close behind the offence. Her husband was rather more indulgent. If something happened at school, he would take the girls' side without any investigation on his part. Bethan wrote of him:

> … [Martyn] *was devoted to the girls … and however busy and hard pressed he was would always have time for them. He would also, it seemed, be as defensive as he dared, on their behalf, when mother was 'laying down the law'!* [3]

Reference was made in an earlier chapter to Mrs Lloyd-Jones' love of poetry. This love of literature was something which she shared with

---

3. Murray (1990), 49.

her husband. (Interestingly, the Doctor's brother Vincent had studied English at Oxford and knew C.S. Lewis quite well.) The Lloyd-Jones' daughters also loved good literature and their parents encouraged them in this. Mrs Lloyd-Jones was very good at finding rare books and passing them on not just to Elizabeth and Ann, but to others. She introduced her children to the Douglas Limberlost books—a genre of Edwardian literature. One of the girls' favourites was, 'A Girl of the Limberlost', which has since been made into a film.[4]

Neither of the girls ever remembers rebelling against their parents: they did not feel there was anything to rebel against. Interestingly, given that the evangelicalism of the early-to-mid-twentieth century was often characterised by 'lists' and 'rules', many of which were both imposed and adopted unthinkingly, Dr and Mrs Lloyd-Jones did not impose a string of rules or laws by which the girls had to abide. Of course, there were certain things to observe, but the Lloyd-Jones' children did not have a harsh or legalistic upbringing. Their mother would merely say, for example, 'You shouldn't play ball—(or such like)—on a Sunday.' As we shall see later in the book, their father was far more relaxed about such things.

The Doctor and his wife always made themselves available for their children, but that did not mean that they did not have time for others. In fact, her own children loved to share their home with friends or members of the church, and this was done in a 'big' way when the girls were younger. Doctor and Mrs Lloyd-Jones for some years had an 'open home' policy for Christmas Day. Martyn, to help his wife, took over the job of the Christmas cards, so that Bethan—ever the perfectionist—could concentrate on hosting a wonderful Christmas. Both Elizabeth and Ann thought Christmas was marvellous and did not mind at all sharing it with others. Like mother, like daughters!

---

4. 'A Girl of Limberlost', a novel written by Genen Stratton-Porter, published in August 1909. Teleplay by Pamela Douglas.

In later life, when it came to Christmases with her grandchildren, Bethan loved every moment. For some years the Lloyd-
Joneses would spend Christmas Day at the Desmonds, the Catherwoods joining them for Christmas dinner, and then New Year's
Day with all the family at the Catherwoods' home in Balsham.[5]
Mrs Lloyd-Jones wrote to a friend saying that they had had a
delightful time with their grandchildren, and that Christmas was
all about the children:

> ... it really *is* their time isn't it. They certainly made the
> most of it!'[6]

Bethan's main aim was bringing enjoyment to others rather than
thinking of herself.

In the Lloyd-Jones household, there was a lovely combination
of having space just for the family and having times when others
were invited in to share. Edith Schaeffer suggests the right balance:

> 'A family is a door that has hinges and a lock.' The hinges should
> be well oiled to swing the door open during certain times, but
> the lock should be firm enough to let people know that the
> family needs to be alone part of the time, just to *be* a family.[7]

If Bethan happened to have a meeting at the church one afternoon,
Martyn would be flexible and rearrange his day so that he could take
the children to school or pick them up at the end of the afternoon.
On those occasions when time was given just to the family, it was
very hard for *some* to bear it if one of the members was missing.
Ann recalls that her father was often 'lost' on a Tuesday afternoon
when her mother went out to take a Bible study. He seemed to her

---

5. Evidently, there was some variation in this practice some years later:
on how the Lloyd-Joneses spent Christmas with their children and grandchildren, see Catherwood (1995), 175–179.

6. Lloyd-Jones Archive: Bethan Lloyd-Jones to friends.

7. Schaeffer (1976), 211.

to 'drift around, just waiting for my mother to return. He was at such a loose end without her'.

Bethan, in her turn, needed her husband as much as he needed her. She watched over her children for their spiritual wellbeing, and if there were any little signs of concern or enquiry into any spiritual matters, she went at once to Martyn to encourage him to take this up with them. But his answer was always the same: 'Spiritual life will come in its own time'. This it did, much to the mutual joy of mother and father. It was with wisdom, the Word and spiritual 'common sense' that Bethan guided her two girls.

'After care'

When Elizabeth and Ann were at Oxford University—Elizabeth in the years 1946–49 and Ann in 1956–59—it was Bethan who wrote such wonderfully 'chatty' letters to them. She was evidently a gifted letter writer. Elizabeth and Ann are agreed in their 'assessment' of this area of their mother's life. 'She was a truly splendid mother. She had a very strong and powerful sense of humour that accompanied her throughout her life and often came out in her letters as well as in her relationships' as her daughters recall.

When the girls reached womanhood and had their own families Bethan still shared in their concerns: they were a very close-knit family. When she invited her children and their families for a meal, her 'perfectionist' strain would rear its head: she would want everything just right for them. They would have to remind her that they were primarily coming to see their parents, and had little concern for how well things looked around the home.

In 1969 the Lloyd-Joneses were in the U.S., and at that time Ann's daughter Elizabeth was unwell and the family doctor diagnosed German measles. Ann was at the beginning of her second pregnancy and, given the effects which can follow for the unborn child of a mother who contracts German measles, she was, quite naturally, concerned. Bethan—ever the letter writer of the two parents—wrote to Ann and her husband, and Elizabeth, alias 'Lisablink' as follows:

(August 12, 1969)

My dearest Keith, Ann and Lisablink,

I do not worry at all about the German measles because if anyone ever had a plastering, you Ann did. It was, I think in 1944, we were all sleeping under that wretched steel table in 2 Colbrook—the Buzzy bombs were non-stop and it was the beginning of July and I was to get away to N.C. Emlyn for the hols—we had less than a week to go and I had just about finished packing when you Ann sickened and blossomed out in the most profuse and convincing rash you ever saw! I tell you, my heart was in my boots and I could not contemplate another 3 weeks of bombs and shelters stretching before us! I remember saying heroically to your father: 'You and Elizabeth must go as planned and Ann and I will follow as soon as she is out of quarantine!!' Then like Christopher Robin, 'All sorts of conditions of famous physicians, came hurrying round at a run.' It was <u>German</u> *measles—all rash and glands! And to crown it all, it transpired that they had changed the quarantine of German measles (28 days in my time!) from 28 to 5 days! Nobody will ever know the relief I felt—I can still feel it now after all these years—and sure enough in 5 days we were—oh so thankfully—crawling down to N.C.E. in those awful wartime trains (Cinderella's chariot for me!!). So you see, though I can forget many things, I can't forget your German measles!*[8]

(Quite apart from the 'family interest' aspect of this letter and what it tells us about Mrs Lloyd-Jones' concern for her family and how it demonstrates her witty way of writing, it is also fascinating for the light which it throws on what it was like living in London under wartime conditions.)

---

8. Lloyd-Jones Archive: Bethan Lloyd-Jones to her daughter Ann.

Then nine days later, from Pensacola in the U.S., came another letter still showing concern and seeking to alleviate any anxiety on Ann's part, who was at this time suffering so much sickness during her second pregnancy and probably still a little apprehensive about the fact that she had been in contact with her daughter, who had had German measles.

August 21, 1969

My dearest Keith, Ann and Bink,
Sorry the sickness is bothersome—these things will <u>not</u> follow the rules and stick to morning, pre-breakfast hours! Let's hope it stops at the end of 12 weeks. I have a theory that I cannot prove, and don't know whether you can positively disprove—that is, that when Bink had 'measles' it was really German measles and that it was she who gave it to the Catherwood 3?! Possible? Of course I did not see her with it—but I was puzzled that if it was measles she had, that she had not been more <u>ill</u> with it. However, it's only a theory and makes no difference to the situation—you have nothing to worry about.[9]

It must have been very difficult for the Lloyd-Joneses, especially Bethan as she had more leisure, being so far away from their family during the very anxious time which Ann and her husband were experiencing. She wrote from abroad:

Dear Keith, Ann and Lizziebinks, who will have quite forgotten us long ago … Thinking no news was good news and hoping there would be a phone call!! We were halfway through dinner when it came!!—your father sitting opposite me, looked quite white (only to my fearful eye, I expect!) and I was rooted to my chair! His side of the conversation soon put me at ease and I could feel waves of real thankfulness washing over me! Good for Bink—and for Dr B too.[10]

---

9. ibid.

10. ibid.

Ann only lived apart from her parents for the four years that she spent in university. In 1965, when she married Keith Desmond, she moved from the family home in Mount Park Crescent, Ealing, London, where the Lloyd-Joneses had lived since 1945. The property in Creffield Road, Ealing to which the young couple moved was sufficiently large for Ann and her husband to live on the first floor, and Dr and Mrs Lloyd-Jones—who no longer needed the large house in Mount Park Crescent—to live on the ground floor.

However, while they were delighted to share the same house with their younger daughter and her husband, the Lloyd-Joneses loved to spend time at Balsham, in Cambridgeshire, where their elder daughter Elizabeth and her husband Fred lived in an old rectory. It was here, in later years, when the Doctor was editing his sermons during his retirement, that they found refuge from the constant demands on the Doctor's time from people—often pastors—who sought his counsel. Although he was still available to respond to various calls, since Balsham was not his home, as Ealing was, he was able to work with fewer interruptions there.

Bethan and Martyn's children, and all their grandchildren, were very close to their hearts. The following accounts indicate how such deep feelings of love and concern were reciprocated by each of them.

Our mother

Both Elizabeth and Ann enjoyed having their parents around them and they look back with gratitude to such wonderful parents and for a mother they loved and cherished, who was such a wonderful role model for them. Elizabeth—Mrs Catherwood—says:

> It's difficult to know where to begin because as far as I am concerned, there could not have been a better mother. Perhaps the best thing I can do is just to enumerate some of her many sterling qualities.
>
> 1) She was a very <u>practical person.</u> Although she maintained that she disliked cooking, she was actually a very good

cook, but what she really enjoyed was cleaning—especially dusting! If she knew visitors were coming, a mini spring-clean would take place while we girls grumbled at the fuss! But it instilled good habits in us.

2) She loved everything to do with <u>language and words</u>. So when travelling abroad she always enjoyed comparing the words used for the same thing in different languages—especially when there was a similarity e.g. church = eglwys in Welsh and église in French—and then realising the derivation of both. She was sensitive, too, to the nuance of a word, which stood her in good stead when she was translating William Williams' Pantycelyn into English and also when she was editing my father's sermons.

She enjoyed doing crossword puzzles and when we were together in Balsham never a day passed but that we had a game of scrabble which she loved and at which she was very good. We always played Lexicon as a family.

She was a good storyteller too—stories about her childhood in Harrow and Newcastle Emlyn; and she could also make up stories—when I had measles, aged six, she kept me going with daily instalments of a story about two little girls and their daily doings.

3) She had a strong <u>sense of humour</u> which often diffused difficult situations and gave us a sense of perspective.

4) Perhaps one of her most outstanding characteristics was her <u>wisdom.</u> This was of inestimable value to her family—husband as well as children—and I myself owe very much because of this. When I was walking in 'the slippery paths of youth' I would consult her and was always grateful for her balanced advice. This gift of hers was invaluable, too, in her role as minister's wife. All kinds of people would seek her advice about all manner of things and found her a great listener full of practical and wise counsel. She spent all day Sunday at Westminster Chapel (where she had an afternoon

Women's Bible Class) and over lunch and tea and at the end of services she was always available to all who wanted to speak to her.

5) She loved her Bible (she used the same one for over fifty years) and was a fount of knowledge for all of us (including my father at times!) on the Old Testament—its teaching, its stories and its people. The latter, you almost felt, she knew as friends, particularly Abraham. She would always sit at a table to read with her Bible before her, and one of my touching memories of her at Balsham is of her sitting like that, reading with her head in her hands and with our old cat sitting in the Bible box on the table beside her. 'Two old ladies together,' she would say.

At this point I feel like the writer to the Hebrews—'And what more can I say ...' Her great physical beauty, her insistence on always dressing well, her determination (she was a strong person), her resolve that her God-given role was 'to keep Martyn in the pulpit', her love for us, her generosity, all these and countless other things make me echo that verse in Proverbs 31: 'Her children rise up also and call her blessed.'

Ann Beatt, Mrs Lloyd-Jones' younger daughter, finds it difficult to find the words to say how much her mother meant to her and her children:

It is not an easy task to write briefly of what my mother meant to me, for two major reasons. Apart from my four years at Oxford, I always lived with her, i.e. for fifty-four years, from my birth in 1937 to her death in 1991; this has made me realise that in a sense the task of biographers is easier, in that they only have access to certain selected facts! My second reason stems from the first—there is too much material, and I find it very difficult to express all that she was to me in comparatively few words.

Polemical writing is not fashionable these days, but I cannot write objectively about either of the most wonderful parents anyone has ever had. I continue to thank God daily for them and even to this day 'Gu & Dadcu' form a large part of my conversation with my children, so that the grandchildren almost feel they knew them as well!

My mother was simply the wisest, funniest, most beautiful woman I will ever know. I know that it is somewhat of a cliché to say that she was 'my best friend', but she fulfilled every definition of this. Throughout my life with her I told her everything, and without her support through some traumatic years I would have been much less able to cope. She was unfailingly wise, calm and unshockable. She also had a way of seeing humour in some of the worst situations and I found this a great help. Many of my friends knew her and almost envied our relationship: several adopted her as their 'confidante' as well, and she was always ready to give them her time, both in person and on the telephone.

She was of course an integral part of my children's lives and they spent almost as much time downstairs with their grandparents as they did with me upstairs. I remember my father saying to me when we bought the house in 1965—'this is an ideal arrangement. If you have children, we can baby-sit and in our old age you can "baby-sit" us'—and that is exactly what happened! It was a comfort to my father as he was dying to know that he was leaving my mother in her own home with us.

After he died, she was never quite the same again, but she derived immense comfort from editing his sermons; she always said that it was the next best thing to having him actually there. She never complained and was always cheerful, loving and as much fun as ever for me and my children. Both of us found it difficult to cry over the really sad things that were happening, but we enjoyed 'having a good cry' over The Waltons or Little House on the Prairie!!

To the end of her life she remained absolutely herself. Her spiritual counsel was as helpful as ever and her physical beauty remained undimmed, so much so that a young nurse in the hospital, on the day of her death, said to me, 'She is the most beautiful woman I have ever seen'.

My father could never really believe that he had 'won' such a wonderful woman, and I can never get over the inestimable God-given privilege of having the two of them as my parents; in Shakespeare's words, 'we shall not see their like again'.

Our grandmother

Bethan's grandchildren loved talking and sharing all manner of things with her: they affectionately called her Gu—a shortened, affectionate form of the Welsh 'mamgu', pronounced 'gee' and 'mamgee', respectively. When they were asked whether they thought their grandfather (Dadcu) or their grandmother (Gu) had the last word, they said, without hesitation, that it was Gu! They all said of her:

She defended her views stoutly against her grandchildren and (they) … remembered her silencing a leading theologian on a point of Christian doctrine.[11]

Christopher Catherwood [1955]—Elizabeth's elder son—writes:

My grandmother kindly took me to the zoo when I was three years old in 1958. I was going to take a ride on an elephant, but when I saw how high up it was I was naturally scared. My grandmother offered to give me a piggy-back ride on her back instead—and fell flat on her nose!

I remember how, when my grandparents stayed at our home in Balsham, she and my mother teamed up together against me and my grandfather to play at least one game of croquet a day. With my grandmother's decades of experience, the women invariably won!

Another clear recollection I have of my grandmother is her reading her Bible at our home—no one knew the Old

11. Catherwood (1996), 209.

Testament as she did. What a wonderful and godly lady she was—but for her husband's unique genius, everyone would have seen how extraordinarily gifted she was in her own right. She was most certainly a fabulous grandmother.

Bethan Marshall [1958], Elizabeth's only daughter, says:

It is impossible to say what influences my grandmother made in just one paragraph. They are too many and too various. What I will say is that my grandmother gave me my name. Like her, I am called 'Bethan' and that gave me an identity which I would not have had otherwise. It made me Welsh. Nowadays Bethan is a much more common name than it was when I was young. Then, it was unusual, and everyone who was not Welsh had various ways of mispronouncing it. I loved putting them straight, a gene I think I inherited from my grandmother. The other thing I liked was telling people that she was the first recorded 'Bethan'. As far as we could tell, no one else was given it before her. That made it not only a Welsh name but a name strongly associated with my grandmother in particular, and that made the name, in my eyes at least, unique. I never called her Bethan of course, but Gu, which is common enough if you are Welsh, but being from west London made me a part of a culture that was bilingual. Of course she was wise beyond measure, a bit of a perfectionist and ruled her household in the manner of the woman in Proverbs, but it is her name that lives on. Bethan.

Jonathan Catherwood [1961], Elizabeth's younger son, shares:

In the early 1970s, when I was a child, I attempted to read the entire Bible in a year. I had been given a Bible by my grandfather, when I was ten years old, with an inscription, '... thanking God that he has already given you the desire to read his Word.'

If truth be told I was more interested in reading the teleprompter on the BBC for the Leeds United results than I was in reading the Bible. Thus my guilt-fuelled attempt. Alas, as often happens, I soon found myself sinking in the quicksand of names, genealogies and rules, which require a steelier sense of purpose than the child-friendly tales of Genesis and early Exodus. When my grandmother was staying with us, I decided to approach her concerning this problem. She was sitting with her Bible in front of her, a fist in each cheek, concentrating as she did on her daily reading.

'Wouldn't it be reasonable', I enquired, 'to just skip the boring bits of the Bible so that one can really get to the heart of the matter?' (I was hoping that the phrase " … getting to the heart of the matter …" would prompt an immediate licence to skip most books.) 'But Johnny', she said, 'We're going to meet all these people one day. What are you going to do when you meet …' and here she paused to consult her Bible—'Obil, who was in charge of the camels?' 'But why would I care that Obil was in charge of the camels?' I protested, sensing glumly that I was not going to get the desired response. 'Well, just think about it', my grandmother continued, 'Camels were an important part of life in the Middle East in those days. They carried water in the desert, they were used in battle, and they could carry goods for trading. Looking after camels was a great responsibility. In fact, it was so great a responsibility that when Obil got the job, they recorded it in the Bible! So, if you skip the book, and never read about him, when you go to Heaven and meet Obil and he says—Did you read about me? What will you say?!'

We laughed, of course, and I wish I could say that I immediately took up reading the whole Bible, but to my regret it wasn't until 25 years later—six years after my grandmother had died—that my guilt finally got the better of me. I tackled the Bible again, but this time armed with the wonderful Murray M'Cheyne scheme of reading the whole Bible in one year. By November, I knew I would achieve my goal. At the end of November, I happened to be in 1 Chronicles 27 verse 30 and read—'Obil the Ishmaelite was in charge of the camels'. Who says that the departed cannot speak to us when they are gone? On that morning I felt the warm smile and wink of my grandmother just one more time.

Liz Desmond [1968], Ann's older daughter, says:

Having always lived with my grandparents, it is very difficult to pinpoint any one particular memory. From the many memories I have of my grandmother, one is when I would watch her making sandwiches for my grandfather when he was travelling somewhere to preach. She would cut the sandwiches up into tiny bite size squares. She explained that she did this so he would be able to carry on reading on the train while he ate.

She was a wonderful grandmother and very much like a second mother to me in many ways. As I grew older, I found myself often going to ask her advice about various things. She was full of wisdom and understanding and was totally un-shockable living in a house with three teenagers.

Rhiannon Tunnicliffe [1970], Ann's younger daughter, shares:

It is difficult to pinpoint particular stories, as she was always just downstairs while I was growing up. One thing that has always stayed with me is, towards the end of her life, she had a fall and broke her wrist. As long as I could remember, she had always worn her hair in a bun during the day and in a plait when she went to bed. She was concerned that, due to her wrist, she would not be able to do her hair. At the time, I too had long hair and reassured her that, as I had watched her putting her hair up and taking it down, my whole life, I knew how to do it just the way she liked it. It was always amusing watching her watching me, like a hawk. It was lovely when I got the second mirror so that she could see how the back looked. She gave me a huge smile and asked me if I wouldn't mind doing her hair every morning and plait her hair every evening before bed. It was a delight to me that she trusted me with her beautiful hair.

During one or two troubled teenage years she was a constant source of loving support, so I felt that I could always tell her anything. I still remember much of her wisdom and miss having her downstairs to go to at a moment's notice.

Adam Desmond [1971], Ann's only son, shares:

I would regularly go downstairs to sit with Gu to watch TV with her and place my feet on her lap, knowing full well that she would immediately start tickling them. I used to watch wrestling on a Saturday afternoon with Dadcu and she would always protest that it was ridiculous. After Dadcu had died, I continued to go in to watch wrestling with her, and she soon started to enjoy it and even had her favourites! On school days she would, without fail, have placed three bright orange vitamin tablets on a chest of drawers in the downstairs hallway near her living room, and upon our return from school there would be three chocolate bars of some description placed where the vitamins once lay. She had a fantastic sense of humour, I could tell her anything and often did. From my first girlfriend to wanting to get a motorbike on my 16th birthday; she took it all in her stride and never seemed to be too shocked by what I told her. When I left home at 17 years, I thought I would never need to go back except on special occasions. The fact of the matter was that I went back almost every day because I missed her beautiful smile and wicked sense of humour so much.

These are wonderful testimonies to a woman who was always accessible to so many people. Some have a different face for those outside the home than for those within it: not so Bethan Lloyd-Jones. Obviously, she had a special love and attention for her own family, but she was always solicitous over the needs of others. Not many can purport to having five generations of Christians within their family, but that is certainly the case in the Lloyd-Jones 'clan'—five generations of people who have, and are, seeking to love and serve the Lord Jesus Christ. Bethan Lloyd-Jones was loved by all her family, and to the wider Christian family she merited the title 'a mother in Israel'.

Love is as strong as death …
Many waters cannot quench love;
rivers cannot wash it away.
Song of Songs 8:6b–7a

Bethan, aged 38 years.

Martyn, Elizabeth, Ann and Bethan. Taken in the summer of 1938,
just before leaving Sandfields.[2]

Ann and Elizabeth, on the steps of St Hilda's College, Oxford. Elizabeth
studied there from 1946-49 and Ann from 1956-59.[2]

Bethan with her family at Balsham, summer of 1976.[2]

Ann and her family - from left to right: Liz Desmond, Adam Desmond,
Ann Beatt & Rhiannon Tunnicliffe.

6

MINISTRY MATTERS

Let the word of Christ dwell in you richly as you teach and admonish one another with all wisdom.
Colossians 3:16

Those who are not looking for happiness are the most likely to find it, because those who are searching forget that the surest way to be happy is to seek happiness for others.
Martin Luther King

Her role

Dr Martyn Lloyd-Jones belonged to a line of illustrious Welsh preachers, a line which stretched back over a number of centuries. One of the great Welsh preachers of the early nineteenth century was John Elias. He was married twice, his first wife having died and thus left him a widower. It would have been difficult for Elias to have accomplished all he did without the support which he received from his first wife. His son wrote of his mother:

My mother endeavoured to take all the cares of the house and business on herself, so that my father's mind should not be

disturbed … her labours in the world were exertions for the
Gospel. [She] proved indeed a helpmeet to him.[1]

John Elias certainly would not have been as useful if his wife
had not been a woman of uncommon energy and prudence. In
the same way, Dr Lloyd-Jones would not have been able to have
accomplished, under God, all that he did, if his wife had not been
the help to him which she proved to be throughout their long years
of marriage. She was the epitome of what a minister's wife should
be. The Doctor was once asked what he believed were the qualities
needed in a pastor's wife. His reply is revealing:

> *What she needs above everything is wisdom, so that she*
> *does not create problems. And another thing is this, she*
> *should never have a special friend in the church. That is very*
> *important. Otherwise it will create division and jealousy. Her*
> *main business is to look after her husband—relieve him of*
> *worries about the home, about food, as far as she can about*
> *financial matters and, very important, not to keep feeding*
> *him with the tittle tattle of the gossip of the church. She is to*
> *protect him and help him.*[2]

Mrs Lloyd-Jones was always available for her husband, seeking to
keep all the domestic ruffles from his world and to free him up
for the work God had called him to do. Her primary domain was
that of wife and mother, and—as we have already seen in earlier
chapters—she delighted in being wife and mother, knowing this to
be her God-given calling. She was fully content with her lot. This, of
course, enabled her husband to be free of certain cares, cares which
might otherwise have been something of a distraction to him in
his gospel work. He once said that he did not mind how great the
pressures were in the ministry, provided that the home was a place
of love, security and peace.

1. Morgan (1973), 76.
2. Murray (1990), 762.

Bethan provided these in abundance. She loved her husband dearly and supported him in all those things which he could do, but she never berated him for the things he could not do. The Doctor knew his limitations: by his own admission, he was the most impractical of men. However, he excelled in the gifts he had received from God: those of preaching, teaching and encouraging. He and Mrs Lloyd-Jones each served God in their own ways.

Having seen Bethan in her role as a wife and a mother, we shall now look at those areas where, in addition to being a support to the Doctor, she made her own contribution to the people of God in the churches where her husband was privileged to serve the Lord.

Minister's wife at Sandfields

In Aberavon, Bethan proved to be a great support to her husband in the visitation work which she undertook amongst the women. Her elder daughter Elizabeth remembers being taken by her mother on the various visits which she made to the women of the church, who preferred, on occasion, to talk things over with her mother rather than with her father. In the church Bethan led a women's Sunday School class for those who were 18 to 30 years old. This was a new experience for her, but she loved every moment of it. Years later she recalled those days:

We chose our book for study, and then we went through it verse by verse. After reading a paragraph or passage—reading verse by verse in turn—each member was encouraged to start us off by asking a question on her verse. They would all talk, discuss and ask and answer questions freely. The time flew by. For some of them it was nothing new, they had always been to Sunday School from their childhood; but for others, newly awakened to spiritual things, it was a new world and they were enjoying having to think. I must add one word on what having that class did for me—it introduced me to the enjoyment of biblical commentaries ... if you are leading a

*class, the more you read the better. I was thus enriched and
far readier to meet the demurring of my class on Sundays.*[3]

Bethan had no favourite themes in the studies and she never used
any 'labels' to describe others. For example, she never said that
a certain Christian was a Calvinist or an Arminian; indeed her
husband—though definitely holding views which are generally
called Calvinistic—never believed that fellowship amongst
Christians should be dependent upon such differences, which
are differences *within* the Christian family. This having been said,
Bethan did not have the theological grasp which her husband
had. While she and the Doctor would discuss various passages of
Scripture, she knew she was no match for her husband—he had a
far greater grasp of theology.

Bethan was certainly very Bible-based, and in the nine years
at Sandfields her class studied Genesis, Matthew, Acts and four
chapters of Hebrews. Mrs Lloyd-Jones had an enormous amount
of pleasure reading through the commentaries and meditating
on God's Word. Her father had not encouraged the use of
commentaries—he believed in 'digging' for oneself—comparing
Scripture with other Scripture passages. Bethan had an astounding
knowledge of the Old Testament, even of its more obscure parts
and characters. As Elizabeth recalls, while her father's knowledge
of the Pauline letters was unrivalled, he would often ask her mother
about the precise location of some Old Testament incident.

Bethan also helped at a ladies' meeting on Thursday afternoons,
where visitors were invited to speak. A Mrs Bradley had inaugurated
this meeting some time before Mrs Lloyd-Jones had arrived at
Aberavon, and she wanted Bethan to have the opportunity of
leading these meetings. Mrs Lloyd-Jones protested strongly,
declaring it to be *this* lady's meeting, but that she would be more
than willing to help in any way she could. Mrs Bradley eventually
agreed! There was such an appetite for spiritual things that some

---

3. Lloyd-Jones (1983), 24–26.

of the women wanted, in addition to this meeting, an extra Bible study during the week. At first, Bethan met these new converts to study and discuss the Bible in her own home, but when the number attending increased considerably, the venue had to be changed to the church. At least one of these women had been converted from a very dark background: she had been a spiritist, who had commanded a considerable fee for her services as a medium, but had been wonderfully transformed by the gospel. Now she wanted to leave behind her even thoughts of such a life:

> ... when asked by Mrs Lloyd-Jones in the course of Bible study in 1 Samuel, what she thought of the action of the witch of Endor in relation to Saul and Samuel (1 Samuel 28), [she] hung her head and confessed that she preferred never to think of such evil any more.[4]

As well as 'dark' lives being changed, there were also some unusual—even 'odd'—people who might wend their way to the church. Indeed, Mrs Lloyd-Jones believed that there was something wrong with a church that did not help and welcome such people. The strangest of these 'odd ones' was an elderly lady who would occasionally attend on Sunday evenings, though she was not a member of the church. She wore an eye patch and seemed quite 'strange and vaguely sinister'. Although Bethan wished to be of help to all people, whether part of the church or not, this lady was someone whom she found she was unable to help. As she was making her way to town one day, she saw the woman leaning against the doorpost of her house, and she beckoned Bethan into her home:

> We sat in her 'parlour'—all very prim and tidy, as indeed, she was herself, with her white hair drawn back severely from her face, and dressed in her usual black with a white collar. She fixed me with her good eye and said, pointing to the eye-shade, 'I want to tell you about this.' I murmured something about

---

4. Murray (1982), 239.

being sorry, and was it a recent accident or something that had happened long ago … She broke across my poor attempt, and said, 'This was not an accident at all. I did it myself.' I gaped at her. She went on, 'Christ says in the Bible that "if thy right eye offend thee, pluck it out and cast it from thee" well, it did offend me and led me into sin, so I did that—'What …?' said I, feebly. 'Yes, I plucked it out and cast it from me. Don't you think I did the right thing?' … I did my best and told her, that if she had only come to Christ in repentance … But she was not listening and did not really want to listen. I left her feeling I had failed her badly, but convinced she was mentally unsound. When, later, I learnt that she had a bad reputation for loose living, I realized once more how the devil takes advantage of the mentally weak. They need our help and our prayers, and to be in a caring, understanding church.[5]

Many of those newborn babes who had been converted found the church at Sandfields to be a caring and understanding community. They had a great desire for the milk of God's Word, and this desire was expressed in their being not only in worship on a Sunday but at the Monday prayer meeting, again at the extra meeting at the manse on a Wednesday, and then on a Thursday afternoon at the ladies' meeting. As well as the Thursday afternoon meeting (which, in those days, was called a 'sisterhood'), there was also a numerically strong 'brotherhood' meeting, which met on a Saturday night. Here, Dr Lloyd-Jones would guide discussion in order to help the men get to grips with the varied problems which they would raise concerning practical aspects of living the Christian life.

One issue which was causing the Doctor particular concern was why there were no babies being born in the church. He soon discovered that the women, for one reason or another, were afraid of having too many children and had therefore stopped having a meaningful sexual relationship with their husbands! The Doctor handed this problem

---

5. ibid., 22–23.

over to his wife, who addressed this matter in the sisterhood meeting. Her medical background proved invaluable in gaining the women's confidence to address with them a subject which, in those days, required far greater delicacy than would be needed today. After this very fruitful discussion which 'Dr' Bethan had with the ladies, the problem was resolved. Soon the sound of babies crying was to be heard in the church! The help which Mrs Lloyd-Jones gave to these ladies was, therefore, in one sense very much of a practical nature. On more than one occasion, the Doctor was to help people by giving advice on such practical matters as how to make a business a success so that bankruptcy could be avoided. All in all, the eleven years at Sandfields were very happy ones: they knew so much blessing during their time at the church. God had totally changed the spiritual atmosphere of the area. Elizabeth, even as a young child, had a sense that God was wonderfully at work in Aberavon: 'When I look back on it,' she recalls now, 'my awareness is of the presence of God ... a sense of glory.' There was a 'radiant sense' in which even a child 'knew that God was there.[6]

Minister's wife at Westminster

Westminster Chapel was, in many ways, a very different church from the Forward Movement Church in Aberavon.[7] Sandfields was

---

6. Catherwood (1995), 47–48. See also Appendix 4.

7. The 'Forward Movement' was the name given to a vigorous evangelistic ministry of the Calvinistic Methodist Church. It began in the late nineteenth century as a result of the spiritual vision of Dr John Pugh, a powerful evangelistic preacher, who was burdened for the industrial, mining, and sea-board towns of South Wales, whose population had increased dramatically as immigrants from Ireland and England (as well as Welsh people from the rural areas of Wales) moved into these towns to find work in the coal mines, and in the case of the sea-board towns, in the docks. At the very beginning it was called 'The Cardiff Evangelistic Movement' and was later re-christened 'The Church Extension and Mission Work'. It was the people who gave it the name 'The Forward Movement' and this is the name that 'stuck'. Many of the largest evangelistic churches in South Wales today began as 'Forward Movement Halls'.

a somewhat deprived area which suffered the ravages of the Great Depression in the 1930s; Westminster Chapel was, by contrast, situated in one of the most sought-after parts of London. At Sandfields, Dr Lloyd-Jones had been sole pastor for the eleven and a half years that he had been there; at Westminster, he was associate pastor with Dr G. Campbell Morgan from 1939 until he became the sole pastor in 1943. While the people at Sandfields were very welcoming of Dr Lloyd-Jones from the outset of his ministry, the situation at Westminster was somewhat different: as Iain Murray points out in his official biography of Dr Lloyd-Jones, there were some, even amongst the church officers, who were not entirely enthusiastic about the Doctor's being there. And finally, whereas Sandfields had been a warm and close-knit fellowship from the very beginning, things were somewhat different at Westminster.

But the Christian life is to be lived out irrespective of place and circumstance, and Mrs Lloyd-Jones displayed the fruit of the Holy Spirit's work in her life as much in her husband's new charge as in the very different circumstances which had prevailed in Sandfields. Although the two situations were very different in some respects, in other respects the church at Westminster called forth some of the same gifts and qualities in her, as a minister's wife, which had been seen in South Wales. At Westminster, for example, as in Sandfields, Mrs Lloyd-Jones' medical opinion was often sought. The Doctor would sometimes suggest that women who had particular problems of a delicate nature speak with his wife. Her training and gifts were never wasted: they were just redirected into different channels. Bethan's medical education and former professional life were invaluable in many ways, although she had pursued this as a career for only a very short period of time. In the medical realm, there was one area where Mrs Lloyd-Jones disagreed with her husband—that was on the topic of homeopathy, one of the forms of what today is categorised as 'alternative medicine'. He accepted some of these methods, while she rejected them outright. But, during an episode of shingles, she was in so much pain that she very reluctantly agreed to take some snake venom! To her great surprise and relief, it worked for her and relieved much of the pain. However, there is no evidence that this single encounter won her over to the whole idea of homeopathy!

When the family moved to Westminster Chapel, the folk there knew nothing of the adult Bible classes which Bethan had led in Sandfields. When, therefore, after the war, the ladies of Westminster Chapel proposed that a ladies' class should be started, Dr Lloyd-Jones was only too pleased for his wife to go ahead and organise one. It was much appreciated by those who met, and continued to be so after Mrs Lloyd-Jones ceased to be the minister's wife there in 1968. Her daughter Elizabeth continued the good work. A certain woman attending the Bible class which Bethan led would often interject during the discussion, 'Mrs. Campbell Morgan would say, "Do this", or, "Do that"', thereby seeking to put one minister's wife at variance with the other. The situation could have been fraught, but Bethan handled it in her own wise way. She did not confront the woman, and eventually such comments petered out.

Mrs Lloyd-Jones was very thorough in her preparation for these classes: it was often very tiring, but the study brought its own reward. The amount of work which the studies necessitated led to her saying on more than one occasion, 'Everyone should be made to teach for two years, never mind National Service!' She did not regard herself, by nature, to be a leader, but women were certainly willing to follow her and obviously benefited greatly from her work, whether that was guidance in study or in any other realm of life: she was always a kind, caring and loving guide to those who sought her help.

Bethan was an invaluable aid not only to the ladies in the church, but also to her husband. The Doctor respected her for her common sense and shrewdness, and put a lot of store by her judgment. One minister recalls her comments on the danger of people flattering a minister: 'Remember that after the "soft soap" comes the close shave!' The Doctor felt his wife was a far better judge of character than he was, and she was proved right nine times out of ten in her assessment of people. The following observation says much for her shrewdness and astuteness in judging character:

> *... when it came to people ... he depended on her very strongly for her assessments of them. Sometimes his enthusiasm would blind him to an individual's defects, whereas she would see through them straight away.*[8]

This does not mean, however, that they always agreed. While he would listen carefully to her views and treat them with the greatest of respect, there were situations where he felt that other considerations were such that he would have to disagree with her. It was while at an early IVF (now UCCF) Conference in Wales that such a difference of opinion occurred. This particular conference was to be remembered for the help which the Doctor's ministry and personal counsel gave to many, not least to those who would later become pastors. He was preaching on the subject of the sovereignty of God, and for the last session was going to speak on this theme as it related to salvation. Inevitably, therefore, the subject of predestination would be considered, 'this high mystery [which] is to be handled with special prudence and care'.[9]

Prudence and care are characteristics not always to be found amongst students, and so it proved on this occasion. While on a coach excursion during the conference, some of the students engaged in cavalier jesting about the topic of predestination, the subject being illustrated by, and compared to, the selecting of gears and the movement of the bus. What made matters worse was that one of the senior men present, who was speaking at the conference and who was already a distinguished medical man himself, took part in the jesting. It was all very clever but also very unspiritual, and the Doctor

---

8. Catherwood (1995), 73.

9. These words come from Chapter III, paragraph VIII of The Westminster Confession of Faith.

was not, as the saying goes, best pleased. At the evening session where he was to speak on this subject the Doctor, in no uncertain terms, rebuked the offenders. As he announced his theme, he heard some repressed laughter. He, therefore, concluded his introductory remarks by saying, 'This is a subject on which you never joke—you do so at your own peril!' The air became 'electric' and the Doctor preached with remarkable power, rapt attention being paid to the message by all who were present. The senior man later apologised to the Doctor, but not before Bethan had voiced her thoughts on the matter to her husband. She felt that the Doctor had demeaned the man in front of others.

'You shouldn't have done that', she said. 'You embarrassed him'.

Mrs Lloyd-Jones empathised with people and in this situation had felt great sympathy for the speaker: she felt that the Doctor should have spoken to the man in private. However, Martyn believed that she had probably been over-sensitive and had responded more in terms of her feelings, rather than out of a concern for a principle.

'The man had made the joke publicly, and therefore needed to be rebuked publicly', was the Doctor's response. Differences of opinion, therefore, could be voiced, but they never spoiled the harmony in the home—or, for that matter, in the church. What is revealing about the Lloyd-Jones' marriage is that the Doctor's belief in male headship in the home did not turn him into some kind of domestic pope or ayatollah—sadly something which has sometimes been done by over-zealous men who have misunderstood the biblical teaching. On the other hand, the Doctor's care for his wife, his encouragement of her to express her opinions and his respect for her views did not make him flinch from standing firm on an issue when he believed that faithfulness to biblical teaching required this. If some men crush their wives, it is to be feared that there may also be men who, out of a misguided concern for their feelings, fail to be true to Scripture. The Doctor seems to have found the right balance in this area.

Mrs Lloyd-Jones helped her husband greatly by sifting a lot of enquirers in the church, and by so doing saved Dr Lloyd-Jones valuable time. She would seek to counsel people herself who, she felt, did not need to see the Doctor. Spending the whole of Sunday at the church, and especially having time to talk with people over lunch, made this kind of ministry quite natural. Elizabeth recalls the very busy Sundays that were spent with so many people at Westminster Chapel. There, assessments and judgments sometimes needed to be made on the spot. There was one woman in the congregation who would not bend her head or her heart with respect to the question of a wife's submission to her own husband. On one occasion she spoke with Mrs Lloyd-Jones, believing herself to have the advantage: 'Are you telling me', she asked, 'that if your husband got you up in the early hours of the morning to post a letter for him, you would submissively obey him?' With characteristic wisdom Bethan replied, 'Oh yes, but as soon as it was morning I'd make sure I made an appointment for him to see the doctor!'

After having spoken with the many who sought his advice after the evening meeting, it was often very late when the Doctor and Mrs Lloyd-Jones were driving their way home through London traffic. Little wonder, therefore, that Mrs Lloyd-Jones sought to be as helpful as she could to her husband in this area of the ministry. Elizabeth remembers how full the day would be for both her mother and father, but they were truly halcyon days for all who were present. Her words give the lie to the oft-repeated charge that Westminster Chapel during the Doctor's ministry was little more than a preaching centre:

We who spent all day Sunday were the Church family, the nucleus who, under God, supported the whole work. So we had our lunch, and talked, and fed strangers, and shared our thoughts and problems … My mother, who was very much at the centre of the time together, always wise, always a good listener, led the Women's Bible Class—talking, encouraging and advising. She was an able lieutenant to her husband, and dealt with many of the problems herself, but always referring to him those she felt needed his particular help. They were great days, and whenever some of us meet again, we always refer to them with gratitude.[10]

Those who regard Westminster Chapel as being little more than a preaching centre during the Doctor's ministry—and there have been not a few who have made this charge—are possibly ignorant of this 'nuclear family' of members and adherents who spent the day at the Chapel, and of the importance of the informal conversations which took place. The idea that the Doctor 'dominated' everything takes no account of this aspect of 'body life' and real fellowship which occurred. And it is clear that Mrs Lloyd-Jones was a key figure in nurturing this aspect of the spiritual life of the church, though she did so in a very natural and unobtrusive way.

Indeed, there are good grounds for believing that the church became *more* of a family during the Doctor's ministry and that Mrs Lloyd-Jones contributed to this development. Adversity often strengthens bonds of fellowship. The war years—and the Doctor became sole minister of Westminster Chapel in 1943—were certainly years of adversity, and in certain respects the life of the church experienced a measure of disruption. But this did much to strengthen the bonds of fellowship amongst those who attended; and, after the family returned to London from Haslemere, Mrs Lloyd-Jones played a significant part in this. The Lloyd-Joneses had a great love for people and enjoyed sharing that love. They operated an 'open-home' at Christmas time for those who had nowhere to go or no one with which to share the celebration: some years there were up to twenty-five or thirty people present with them at Christmas. In 1944 one young woman, far from home, joined the Lloyd-Jones family to celebrate Christmas. She wrote home to her family in the U.S.A. to describe her day with them:

Their dining room was nicely decorated for the season and we had a fine dinner of goose—with all the trimmings—followed

10. ibid., 73.

by two hot Christmas puddings. They put 'prizes' in their puddings, as we do in wedding cakes, and I drew a duck and a thrupenny bit, which I shall bring home with me as souvenirs of the occasion … After dinner we talked a while, listened to the King's speech, and then started to play games. We played all sorts of games—some old, some new, and everybody played—from seven year old Ann to her grandmother and everybody in-between. We all laughed uproariously and had a marvellous time … For supper we had cold goose, vegetables, assorted cakes and tea. Ann came in dressed in a Santa Claus suit and gave us all little presents from her pack. After supper we sang, around the piano. Carols first and then Welsh hymn tunes … And so endeth the story of my Christmas—a very happy one, thanks to some very fine people.[11]

The war years must have been a very unsettling time for the congregation at Westminster Chapel. They were quite literally taking their lives in their hands in attending the church. And yet, of course, they were not: the words, 'my times are in *His* hands' must have regularly sprung to mind. Elizabeth recalls:

My mother has many memories of going to church in wartime. Another flying bomb landed even nearer to the Chapel, and this made the fabric unsafe. The congregation had to go for a while to nearby Livingstone Hall … and the sense of danger from the unpredictable bombs was ever present. But our sense of fellowship was very strong, and though few in number and in somewhat depressing surroundings, we still knew the presence of the glory of the Lord.[12]

Although Mrs Lloyd-Jones played a significant part in encouraging and nurturing fellowship within Westminster Chapel, she had no special friendships within the church: she was very careful

11. Murray (1990), 121–22.

12. Catherwood (1995), 63.

about this because she felt it could cause jealousy amongst some, and breed pride in others. She made herself equally available to everybody in the church. Most of her close friends were not drawn from either of the churches of which the Doctor was minister. However, it would appear through the numerous letters she sent to some in Westminster Chapel that she had a special affection for a number who were very helpful and solicitous over her welfare.

There was a very different approach to the visitation of the congregation in London from that which had obtained at Sandfields. The people attending Westminster were widely scattered: attendees came from various suburbs of London and even further afield. Most of Bethan's 'pastoral work' amongst ladies was done by sending thoughtful notes or cards to those who were poorly, or in need and confined to their homes. She carried many on her heart and in her prayers, and embraced many people in this way. And her care and concern for people continued even after they had moved to another area. The following extract is from a letter, written in February 1963, to a lady who had been a member of the Sunday afternoon Bible class which Mrs Lloyd-Jones led. She had moved to another area to live and, in the exceptionally heavy winter of 1962–63,[13] this lady had broken her wrist. The letter is a model of natural, pastoral care for someone who was no longer at Westminster:

> *My dear Miss Harris,*
> *Have been meaning to write to you for a long time, but 'meaning to write' somehow or other never writes letters!! I am so sorry, because I wanted you to know that all of us— your friends at Westminster—were really concerned and sorry to hear of your fall & your broken wrist. I am sure it has been a real trial to you, because it is really depressing to have to depend on friends and neighbours for every little job—little jobs that are done almost without thought—& then*

---

13. The snow had begun to fall the day after Christmas Day, and in many parts of the country it was still on the ground a number of months later.

suddenly, you just can't do them—getting into a belt, fastening suspenders, buttoning buttons!!! Oh dear! I'm sure you must have groaned out your impotence many a time, beside the pain which you must have endured. There have been quite a few falls & breakages among our members—another broken wrist—one sprained, one broken thigh, one badly bruised face … it has been terribly treacherous under foot … We never saw a blade of grass in this garden for 6 weeks and the poor birds—! … I used to think snow is so pretty!!! At first—the first Sunday after Christmas especially—our congregation suffered badly—no buses running, car drivers afraid to venture out, all the train services hopelessly disorganised—some services only running one train an hour! The congregation was very small—smallest we've seen since the war.[14]

This young lady was finding it hard to settle in her new church. Mrs Lloyd-Jones was obviously still concerned and had remained in touch with her. The letter continues:

I do hope that underneath different methods and other ways, you have by now found the same love to the Lord Jesus Christ, the same spirit of worship and the same joy of salvation as we knew together for the past three years of happy fellowship. May God bless you & give you always a sense of His nearness.

Hoping your poor wrist is nearly as good as new by now & with the prayerful interest & remembrance of all your friends at Westminster—the Bible Class in particular.

> *With my love.*
> *Affectionately*
> *Bethan Lloyd-Jones.*[15]

This letter is interesting for a number of reasons. First, it is clear that Mrs Lloyd-Jones' Christian love and concern for people was

---

14. Lloyd-Jones Archive: Bethan Lloyd-Jones to Miss Harris.

15. ibid.

not something which she affected, nor was it something which she viewed as part of the 'professional duty' of a minister's wife: she was still concerned for this sister in Christ after she had moved from the area and was attending another church. Secondly, the following words from the letter reveal something of Bethan's generous catholicity of spirit:

I do hope that underneath different methods and other ways, you have by now found the same love to the Lord Jesus Christ, the same spirit of worship and the same joy of salvation as we knew together for the past three years of happy fellowship.[16]

In the early 1960s Westminster Chapel was, if not unique, still quite different from much of 'mainstream' evangelical life in much of Britain. Bethan was evidently aware of the fact that Miss Harris might well find it impossible to find a church which did things in a similar way to the way in which they were done in 'the Chapel'. What was important to Mrs Lloyd-Jones, however, was not so much the methods and ways—these could, indeed, be 'different methods and other ways'—but 'the same love to the Lord Jesus Christ, the same spirit of worship, and the same joy of salvation'. In this, of course, Bethan was similar to her husband: although he had his convictions as to 'how things should be done', he was always concerned about 'the big things' of the gospel, such as love to Christ, the *spirit* of worship and the joy of salvation. It is a pity that in recent years some who have been admirers of the Doctor as well as some of his critics have assumed that he was more concerned about 'methods and ways' than the 'big things'. His wife understood him so well and shared his vision for the big things: there was nothing mean, small-minded or petty about her.

In addition to hospital visits and letters which she wrote, Bethan spent hours on the phone with individuals, many of whom were suffering from depression and who needed a listening ear. She

16. ibid.

loved people and being involved in the needs of families who came to her. But whatever the needs they had, she would not wrongly criticise anyone, nor would she speak of them to others. Sometimes there may have been someone in the church who may have been 'difficult', and Bethan might say to her family, 'I'll tell you all about it one day.' She never did!

Wider ministry

Like various men in history—one thinks of someone like Spurgeon—Dr Lloyd-Jones' ministry was much wider than being the pastor of Sandfields, then of Westminster Chapel. The range of gifts with which God had endowed him meant that he ministered throughout the country and also in other parts of the world. One area where his wider ministry was particularly valued was that of being an advisor or counsellor to other ministers—*pastor pastorum*, a pastor of pastors. But it was no less the case that Mrs Lloyd-Jones exercised a similar ministry to the wives of ministers. Her advice to one such lady was to prove to be of incalculable blessing to the cause of the gospel in Wales.

From the late 1940s a significant work of God had begun in Wales, largely as a result of a remarkable IVF campaign held in Llanelli, South Wales in 1945 and of a work of God's Spirit amongst students in North Wales, especially between 1945 and 1948.[17] These two tributaries of God's work were eventually to run into one course, which would become known—at the suggestion of the Doctor, who became closely identified with what was going on—as *The Evangelical Movement of Wales*.[18] From the early 1950s onwards its ministry grew: over the years, and still today, it has held separate annual conferences in Welsh and English, separate

---

17. See Fielder, 108–148.

18. For more background information and the history of *The Movement* or the *EMW*, as it is generally known amongst Christians in Wales, see especially Davies (1984) and Gibbard (2002). Information is also to be found in Fielder (1983) and Murray (1990).

ministers' conferences in the two languages, ministers' fraternals, and summer camps for children and young people. *The Movement* also manages a publishing work which, in addition to publishing various books—some being translations from Welsh undertaken by Mrs Lloyd-Jones—produces a Welsh and an English magazine. Furthermore, it supports and organises a residential theological training course, which has literally prepared scores of men for gospel ministry from England, Wales, Scotland and Ireland. Inevitably, an army of people has been involved in this work, some ministers having been heavily identified with its ministry, and, in addition to having been used in their own churches, have been a means of spiritually enriching the lives of many beyond their immediate home church or base.

Although Wales is a small country, one man who was heavily identified with this work of God travelled extensively throughout the Principality for many years and this, as with the Doctor, meant that he was regularly away from home. His itinerant ministry was of incalculable spiritual blessing to many, and it was this which created something of a dilemma for his wife. She was aware of the way in which God was using her husband but was concerned at the effect that his absences from home might have upon their children. She shared her concern with Mrs Lloyd-Jones. Her counsel proved to be of great help and value: 'Talk often of your husband to them and of the importance of his work.' How many Christians, pastors, and churches—as well as her own children—benefited from this advice, as this minister's wife continued to give her husband up to the work to which he had been called! Indeed, he would not have travelled as frequently as he did had his wife not encouraged him to do so. As a result the cause of Christ in Wales benefited greatly, and this as an indirect result of the counsel given by Mrs Lloyd-Jones.[19] In this case, of course, the advice was drawn from her own experience.

19. The information was given to the author in a personal interview with the lady concerned, who has specifically asked not to be identified.

On another occasion Bethan was asked by the same lady for advice, but this time the counsel that was to be given was not from Bethan's own personal experience. A tradition had grown up in many chapels in Wales that a minister's wife should never work outside the home. However, this particular lady felt a measure of conflict in herself because she believed that it would be necessary to supplement her husband's income, which was not sufficient for their growing family, and this could be achieved by her going out to work. Therein lay her dilemma: it seemed sensible to take on a job, but this would be going against the prevailing 'fashion' for a minister's wife.

When Bethan was at their home while Martyn was preaching in the vicinity, this lady asked Mrs Lloyd-Jones' opinion as to whether or not she thought a minister's wife should work. 'There is nothing wrong with someone wanting to help the family economy, as long as the family does not suffer', was Bethan's comment on the subject. Mrs Lloyd-Jones was never wrongly judgmental of others: although she herself had not needed to work to supplement the family income, she certainly did not frown upon this woman's inclination to take paid employment. In fact, she encouraged and commended her for seeking to help her family in their need, much to this wife's relief and comfort. She took a job, and the children certainly did not suffer because their mother was always there at the beginning of the school day and when they returned home at the end of the day.

Thus, if Barnabas was a son of encouragement, Mrs Lloyd-Jones was a 'daughter of encouragement'. The fact that she encouraged this lady in this particular way, at a time when in Wales it was not quite 'the done thing' for a minister's wife to take outside employment, demonstrates that she thought things through for herself and did not merely follow human tradition: she was quite prepared to give advice which broke with tradition and contradicted it. She was a woman who sought to base her convictions on the Word of God rather than upon the opinions of men. One thinks, in this connection, of the 'wife of noble character' of Proverbs 31: evidently she was a woman who had an economic input into her family (vv. 16–17), but far from compromising the general welfare of the family, it is clear that the family life was enhanced—both her children and her husband heaped praises upon her head (v. 28), and her value was, 'far above rubies'. (v. 10.)

At times, some feminists have tried to caricature the position of those who hold to biblical teaching on male and female role models, seeking to stereotype it as keeping the woman in the kitchen and making her economically dependent upon her husband, and as not having a mind of her own. We have seen earlier on that Mrs Lloyd-Jones did her own thinking and was encouraged to do so by her husband. The example of the advice which she gave to this particular minister's wife amply demonstrates that, at a time before feminism had made significant strides, Mrs Lloyd-Jones did not fit into any stereotypical mould. She was concerned that the counsel which she gave to others would express the wisdom which is from above rather than merely reflecting whatever happened to be the prevailing view in the world at large or in the evangelical world at the time. How appropriate it was, therefore, that as she was such a great help to her husband in his ministry, she owed not a little of her ability to give Bible-based counsel to others to his influence upon her! Incidentally, it may not be amiss to point out that the wife of John Elias—to whom reference was made earlier—kept a shop in the early nineteenth century to help with the family income, so that he could devote himself more wholeheartedly to the work of the gospel.

As we conclude this part of the portrait, in which we have considered her role as the wife of a very busy minister, it will be appropriate to consider Mrs Lloyd-Jones' response to a question she was once asked as to how she was able to cope with the demands that her husband was under, in being available to so many people, and the impact which this inevitably made upon her own life. Her reply, quite simply, was that she considered it the greatest privilege

of her life to be married to such a godly man. Bethan Lloyd-Jones—
always so self-effacing!

We have not stopped praying for you and asking God to fill you with the knowledge of his will through all spiritual wisdom and understanding. And we pray this in order that you may live a life worthy of the Lord and may please him in every way …
COLOSSIANS 1:9–10a

Bethan Lloyd-Jones' Sunday School class at Sandfields.[1]

Westminster Chapel.[1]

7

OVER TWENTY YEARS OF LIFE

Religion that God our Father accepts as pure and faultless
is this: to look after ... widows in their distress.
JAMES 1:27

Kindness is a language which the deaf can
hear and the blind can see.
MARK TWAIN

The widows

Magdalene Lloyd-Jones—Martyn Lloyd-Jones' mother—was both a forceful and resourceful individual. When Martyn was only fourteen his father bade a temporary farewell to his family in order to look for work in Canada, the intention being that Magdalene (known as Magdalen by the family) and her sons would later join him. This difficult and trying period had arisen as a result of the family business having to be sold—together with the home in Cardiganshire—because of financial difficulties into which it had fallen. Magdalen—or Maggie, as she was also known—was left caring for the children and the home. With no prospect of work materialising in Canada, and after a very real struggle, Henry Lloyd-Jones decided that there was no future for his family there, and he made plans to return home and start life again in London. He informed his wife of this and suggested that she try to arrange for him to stay with relatives in London so that he would have a base to look for employment. It must have been a very stressful time for Maggie, especially in view of the fact that two of their boys were sitting exams at the time. In a letter to his wife and children Henry wrote as follows:

> *I very much hope you will be able to hit on something in London very soon, I do not think it is any use thinking of staying here … Please do not lose any time as I am getting so uneasy. … I do hope you can get something in London.*[1]

One would have to be resourceful in such a situation, and Magdalen Lloyd-Jones proved that she was. The Lloyd-Jones family did end up in London, and it was through that decision, humanly speaking, that Martyn and Bethan met! Circumstances were very trying for some time, but Martyn's parents were eventually able to buy a dairy business. Although the business proved to be a success and the Lloyd-Jones' financial troubles were put behind them, it was nevertheless the case that at this time Henry Lloyd-Jones and Tom Phillips lived in very different worlds—and so did their children, the only place where social contact was made between them being in the Welsh Calvinistic Methodist Church at Charing Cross.

Henry Lloyd-Jones, 'one of nature's gentlemen', died in 1922, leaving his beloved Magdalen a widow for twenty-nine years. Until she eventually went to live with the Doctor and his family, Martyn kept up a regular correspondence with his mother throughout the years of her widowhood, especially on the anniversaries of the deaths of his father and of his brother Harold. This was certainly so when his mother was absent from London—whether this was when she was away on holidays or visiting friends or family, or whether it was after she finally left her home in London to go to live back in her home area in West Wales. But she did not end her

---

1. Murray (1982), 29–30.

days in Wales. The last years of her life she was to spend living with her son Martyn and his family.

Mrs Lloyd-Jones senior was by no means as gentle a person as her husband had been! In fact she was quite the opposite. However, Bethan managed to keep everyone happy and contented within the home, and she was as concerned about her mother-in-law's well-being as she was for that of her own mother. Bethan never complained about her change of circumstances, although at times it could not have been easy to *juggle* young and old alike. Then, on the 22 June, 1951, at the age of 79, Magdalen Lloyd-Jones left this world and was buried in Llandyfriog, her home area.

As one door closed, another one opened. In 1952 Bethan's mother came to live with her in the family home at Ealing. Tom Phillips and his wife had moved back to 'Sunnyside' in Newcastle Emlyn during the Second World War and had continued to live there after the war ended. Dr Phillips died in 1947 aged 87 and Mrs Phillips, having lived for a while with a cousin, eventually went to live with the Lloyd-Joneses. Three generations were, therefore, living under one roof. Ann, a young teenager at the time, loved her grandmother but was nevertheless somewhat frightened of her, finding her somewhat strict and forbidding. Elizabeth, nine years her sister's senior, had a different view of her maternal grandmother—she loved her without the fear. And Bethan? In spite of the fact that her childhood had been very happy indeed, her relationship with her mother having been a warm one, she did not feel at liberty to share very much of herself with her mother. But in another sense she certainly did share herself, and her home, with her: having 'taken in' her mother-in-law for some years, she now 'took in' her own mother for nine years. And this involved far more than simply having her live with the family.

There was the practical concern as to the future of Sunnyside. The summer of 1954 saw Bethan 'spring cleaning' after her elderly uncle and the family maid, Hilda, had died that year. She wrote as follows to friends:

My dear Mr & Mrs Secrett,

The days which have been jogging along in a very pleasant leisurely way are now pricking up their ears & beginning to gallop, & we realise with quite a sense of shock that it is three weeks yesterday since we left home! Of course the first week included three days of really whole time spring cleaning of mother's little home in N.C. Emlyn. We had quite a job with the house …[2]

Then in July of 1955 Bethan 'set to' again—this time with a vengeance! On this occasion it was not just a 'summer' clean, but a wholesale clearing and cleansing of the property. This Bethan took upon herself with great alacrity! The house had been empty for eleven months. This is how she described things to the Secretts:

… it needs someone in residence to see that it gets its nourishment little & often! Anyway, believe me, it got a good do this time … We turned out more stuff than you would think it could hold, & the Aunts, Uncles and maid had long before they died become quite decrepit, & had certainly turned nothing out for the past 50 years or so, the moth and rust had made the most of their opportunity! Added to this, the Uncle who was the last survivor of the family, had a bee in his bonnet about <u>dust</u>. Dust must on no account be disturbed!! If anyone touched a duster he immediately got a cold & a temperature & was (professedly) very ill! By the time he died last August, the ancient maid had quite caught the idea & the home-help provided by the large-handed council at 30/- a week did nothing but make the fires, the meals & wash the front door step! The state of things was incredible. The aforementioned home-help & her husband (garage-hand) took away cartloads of rubbish with instructions to distribute anything possible to the oldest inhabitants, & to take the rest

2. Lloyd-Jones Archive: Bethan Lloyd-Jones to her friends, the Secretts. 13 August 1954.

to a nearby field, pour a bottle of petrol & oil over it & put a match to the lot—which they did!! The home-help scrubbed for us and we left the place smelling quite healthily of carbolic and Stergene! By the time we finished we only had one idea of luxury—a hot bath. I had thought of washing out the residue dust of Sunnyside from my hair in Liverpool. There was such a drought and dearth of water in the farm that I couldn't even suggest it there. When we got to Liverpool it was hot & sticky beyond description & I could not get my hair washed— despair! We had quite a good crossing & there in Belfast at 9.00 a.m., in the most primitive place imaginable, I got a nice little Irish girl to do it. I had to go out into the passage to sit to have it dried because the flex wouldn't reach!!![3]

The Lloyd-Jones' summer holidays at Newcastle Emlyn came to a close, therefore, in the July of 1955. As she shut the door of Sunnyside, it brought to a close 95 years of someone in her family living under that roof—the home that had been 'like a public house without the beer'.

Margaret Phillips continued to live with the Lloyd-Joneses for another six years after this, but it was at her son Ieuan's home that she ended her days, when she was visiting there in 1961. She had lived to the good old age of ninety-three—the days, in fact, that would be allotted (all except for a few months) to her own daughter Bethan. With Mrs Phillips' passing came the end of a whole generation in the Lloyd-Jones/Phillips family and also the end of an era.

> *Your attitude should be the same as that of Christ Jesus:*
> *who, being in very nature God … made himself nothing,*
> *taking the very nature of a servant …*
> PHILIPPIANS 2:5, 6a, 7a

---

3. Lloyd-Jones Archive: Bethan Lloyd-Jones to her friends, the Secretts. 29 August 1955.

Three generations:
Bethan with her mother and Elizabeth.

Four generations: Bethan with Elizabeth,
her grandson Christopher and her mother.

8

WONDERFUL WAY WITH WORDS

*She opens her arms to the poor
and extends her hands to the needy.*
PROVERBS 31:20

Joy is increased by spreading it to others.
ROBERT MURRAY M'CHEYNE

Helping the needy

Bethan Lloyd-Jones made a real contribution to some of the 'elderly babes' who were converted at Sandfields. Mark McCann was one such older convert. He was in his early sixties and the chief love of his life had been to go from one fair to another simply to enjoy a good fight! He had an extraordinarily large moustache that was waxed and which extended beyond each ear-lobe. Indeed, such was its length that he referred to it as his 'moustaches'. He was exceedingly proud of this 'specimen' and would have fought to the death to defend his title of having the longest moustache in Wales. McCann was known as 'the Devil's General', and men knew how to raise his ire. Someone had but to say that another man had a bigger or better moustache and then, usually already 'well oiled' with drink, McCann would give in to his uncontrollable temper and would literally go berserk, nearly killing the man who had dared to make such a claim. Bystanders would usually flee the scene. Mrs Lloyd-Jones later recalled:

> *Mark McCann once gave me another terrible illustration of this insane temper. He had come in for his dinner one day and his well-filled plate was on the table. He stopped to wash his hands in the outer kitchen and when he got to the table he found the dog eating his dinner! He told me—with bowed head and averted eyes—that he took that dog out to the kitchen sink and cut its head off with a bread knife! These things were told … with deep shame … muttered in a low voice as though he must tell the worst and be reassured again of the everlasting mercy.*[1]

The first night he was brought to church, he was converted! He could not, however, bring himself to remain after the meeting. (It was customary at Sandfields for there to be a second 'after meeting' at which those who had come to faith remained and confessed to the church their newfound faith.) An endless week followed, at the close of which he was able to tell what God had done for him, and he afterwards wished that he had had the courage to remain and tell out his soul the week before. The church rejoiced with Mark McCann, and gloried in the opportunity of caring for and loving this 'babe' in Christ.

Some weeks after his conversion, he came into church with his 'moustaches' having been shaved off and in *their* place there was but an 'ordinary and unobtrusive substitute on his upper lip'. Dr Lloyd-Jones was concerned that someone had been bringing pressure to bear upon this young Christian, but Mr McCann's response was:

> *… nobody told me to do it … it was one morning when I was shaving, and I looked at myself in the mirror, and I looked at my moustache, and I said to myself—them things isn't for*

---

1. Lloyd-Jones (1983), 71–72.

Christians, and I cut it off … as he learned of other things
which 'isn't for Christians', they had to go.[2]

Mark McCann had had very little formal education. One evening as Mrs Lloyd-Jones was leaving the church, she passed a group of men standing with Mark McCann. They shared with her the problem which he had: he could not read. Now that he was converted, he had an insatiable desire to read the Scriptures. Bethan was always eager to be of help to those in need. She knew that it was easy enough to teach a child to read, and with great confidence declared that if he wished, she would help him. She remembered her mother doing just the same thing many years before at Harrow with an elderly gentleman named Mr Matthews:

In no time at all Mr Matthews was reading, slowly and
haltingly at first with a finger picking out the words, but
soon with ease and great delight. When he first picked out
the word Iesu (Jesus) he broke down completely, and with
tears running down his cheeks, and crying, 'Oh, his name, his
blessed name!', he picked up the book and kissed that name.[3]

What Bethan had forgotten, however, about her mother's teaching of Mr Matthews was that she had taught him to read through the medium of Welsh, and Welsh is a wonderfully phonetic language. Not so easy for Mr McCann in English! On her fourth attempt at *The Little Red Hen*, a children's book, she felt rebuked when Mark McCann said:

… half apologetically and half rebelliously, 'I don't want to
read that, I want to read the Bible! …'[4]

And that is what they did! The work was painstaking but rewarding and did eventually achieve its goal. Mark McCann did read John's Gospel and 'his joy knew no bounds and transformed his idle days'.

2. ibid., 75–76.

3. ibid., 78.

4. ibid., 79.

Letters to family and friends

Holidays were not for Bethan a time when she would forget about friends; on the contrary, she wanted to share with them even though she was apart from them. She would send 'newsy', informative letters. On one occasion she and the Doctor had a short break in Wales before holidaying in Ireland. Here is an extract from a letter which she wrote to their friends Mr and Mrs Secrett, before leaving for Ireland, sharing with them her disappointment at the way the gospel had been preached. (Mr Secrett became a very good and trusted deacon at Westminster Chapel.) The direct proclamation of the gospel was very important to Bethan:

We had quite an interesting time on the Sunday, slipping into the back seat of the Welsh Baptist Church to hear a very popular Welsh Baptist preacher of the old school, about the last of the barons I should think, a Mr Jubilee Young, slight ... interesting looking—with a strong look of Dr C.M. on a small scale—the philosophical type, delightful, endearing and good preaching to the children in the morning—totally uninspired in the evening. Everything right and good <u>about</u> the Gospel, but never the direct preaching of it and nothing to convict anyone. Congregation—poor.[5]

In the same letter we discover what the Lloyd-Joneses thought of the cinema. They were due to meet Ann in the early afternoon at Liverpool railway station before they would all travel on together, later in the evening, to Ireland. Having time on their hands, Ann encouraged them to go to the cinema with her to see *The Robe*, a Hollywood 'religious epic'. Bethan shared her thoughts with the Secretts after seeing the film:

We were not due on the boat until about 8.30 & were wondering how to fill in our time, but Ann decided for us! ... she prevailed upon Martyn to come and see it. It certainly made the time

5. Lloyd-Jones Archive: Bethan Lloyd-Jones to the Secretts.

*fly—it is a wonderful piece of work and very well done, but
Martyn says, he can't see Cinema as the vehicle of spiritual
truth, religious films notwithstanding and however good. I was
relieved and thankful for the obvious sensitiveness, reverence
and good taste evinced towards the incidents in the Life of our
Lord, which were shown as bearing on the story. But it must
be a grave spiritual danger to the actors <u>acting</u> the tremendous
things they were supposed to be feeling and experiencing. M
& I had not been to a cinema together (me not at all I think)
since we saw Charlie Chaplin in The Great Dictator during the
war. There was an air-raid warning during the performance
and I was filled with horror at the thought of being bombed
in a Cinema.*[6]

It is interesting to note Bethan's shrewdness in correctly assessing
the spiritual danger of acting the tremendous things which the
actors were supposed to be feeling and experiencing. The part of
Marcellus—the Roman tribune who in the film executes Jesus,
is later moved to repentance and becomes a Christian, and
subsequently dies a martyr's death—was played by Richard Burton.
The most recent—and certainly the largest and surely the most
definitive biography of Burton—refers to the two affairs which
Burton was running on set with two women![7]

In another letter to Mr and Mrs Secrett, this time written from
South Africa in 1958, Bethan described the 'Knob Church': both
the building and the preacher's theological stance. She could be as
perceptive in her views on preaching as she was with respect to the
spiritual dangers of acting out spiritual realities:

*… aesthetically most beautiful and must have cost many
fortunes e.g. it is carved all over and stained glass all over
and every inch of carpet all over. I believe it is evangelical <u>in</u>*

---

6. ibid.

7. Rubython (2011), 270

intention but it does seem to me that evangelicals are so sorely lacking in knowledge and theology that they have very little *discernment* and they are able to 'pass' men and sermons and various writings which I should feel to be more than doubtful and judge them by what they say rather than by what they *don't* say, so that if they don't say anything wrong they are judged to be right![8]

While abroad, Mrs Lloyd-Jones always remembered her Women's Bible Class at Westminster Chapel. She sent them very informative letters, often making reference to her husband's preaching, and she regularly gave quite detailed descriptions of the interior of various churches which they visited. At her last meeting as their leader, the ladies in her class had presented Bethan with a parting gift before she left for what was her and Martyn's longest visit to the U.S. in 1969. She wrote:

April 19, 1969—Jenkintown.
To the Bible Class.

My dear friends all,
Here I am fulfilling my promise to write to you from America
… the evening service … was to start (unusually) at 4.0!
This was to be a lecture … In the end, of course, it was a
straightforward service, as any 'lecture' of Dr's always turns
out to be a sermon—and so it was with this. I felt there was
great freedom and power in the service and you could have
heard a pin drop … By the way, it was the plushiest and most
ornate church I have ever been in. Huge interior with pillars
and stucco decorations lavished all over everything, enormous
domed head-room with coloured glass and everything painted
white—thick crimson carpet and background to the pulpit
and all the pews with not only deep luxurious scarlet cushions,
but the backs as well! … Well, dear, dear friends, I must stop

8. Lloyd-Jones Archive: Bethan Lloyd-Jones to the family.

now ... my little clock is a constant companion and is as reliable as Big Ben! It never gains or loses a second, and its alarm is enough to make us jump out of our very skin! It is a very precious possession not only for its own sake, but for what it stands for. I couldn't say anything of what I truly felt at our lovely party—my heart was too full, I didn't even thank you properly for party or the gift, but I do thank you now ... what can I do now but assure you of my undying affection in deep gratitude for your loving fellowship over the years and to pray God's abundant blessing on you and your new leader!!!

With my fondest love and happy memories in abundance, Affectionately Bethan Lloyd-Jones.[9]

(The three exclamation marks with reference to the new leader were placed there because the new leader was to be her own daughter Elizabeth.)

At the end of many of the letters she sent to the Secretts, Bethan often wrote: 'Well my dears, we ... send you our love and warmest remembrance and <u>mind don't forget us while we are away.</u> Ever most affectionately, Bethan Ll-J'.

Text messaging is, no doubt, a wonderful means of instant communication in the modern world. It may come, however, at a price, and a very heavy price at that: the 'art' of letter writing may well be disappearing from the earth. It is undoubtedly the case that some people seem to have been blessed with a gift for letter writing, and Bethan Lloyd-Jones was certainly one such individual. Her higher education had been in the medical sciences, but her letters reveal a woman who evidently loved language and who had a wonderful way with words. On a small card to the Secretts she included a description of the foggy weather which they had experienced while sitting and waiting for six hours to land off the coast of Ireland:

---

9. Lloyd-Jones Archive: Bethan Lloyd-Jones to her Bible Class at Westminster Chapel.

Well, my dears ... (a nice calm sea) except the weather which draped grey veils in infinite variety all over the scenery. Still a feast for the eyes, but rather uncomfortable—condensing in cold drops down the back of the neck! [10]

While on their annual holiday, whether abroad or in Britain, Bethan would often write letters to the Secretts in which she would acquaint them with all that she and her husband were doing. Bethan never forgot Mr and Mrs Secrett's birthday or wedding anniversary, and even when she was abroad she sent telegrams with good wishes for such occasions. The caring and sharing were obviously reciprocal: there were many letters and gifts which found their way into the Lloyd-Jones' home. We know from Bethan's correspondence that one of her gifts was a kitchen timer. She wrote on a 'Thank You' card:

I do thank you with all my heart for your loving thought of me on my birthday, and I am so delighted to have a new 'Dinger'—the one I have is old and erratic (like me!!!) and likely to let me down at any time—no excuses now for 'forgetting the oven'!' Thank you very, very much and for all that friendship means <u>all</u> of the time. My fondest love to you both, affectionately, Bethan Lloyd-Jones. [11]

We have seen earlier that Mrs Lloyd-Jones avoided making special friends in the two churches of which her husband was the minister. The letters to and from the Secretts, however, indicate that this statement needs to be qualified somewhat. The Secretts took a genuine and practical interest in the Lloyd-Jones' welfare: on one occasion Mr Secrett, who was a builder, helped find a property for them to live in. Given the genuine kindness and consideration which the Secretts showed to their minister and his wife, there would have been a lack of basic courtesy and gratitude if this had not been acknowledged by the Lloyd-Joneses.

10. Lloyd-Jones Archive: Bethan Lloyd-Jones to the Secretts.

11. ibid.

Quite naturally, therefore, something of a close bond developed between them. Indeed, this was not unrelated to the fact that Mr Secrett was evidently a very warm, spiritually minded man, whose general theological outlook—that of Calvinism, since he had come from a Strict Baptist background, which would have been Calvinistic—coupled with his warm spirituality was a tremendous encouragement to the Doctor in the very early years of his ministry at Westminster.[12] However, it is clear that both the Secretts and the Lloyd-Joneses were very discreet, as were other members of the church with whom friendships were built over the years, and these relationships did not create difficulties for the way the Lloyd-Joneses related to the rest of the church, or the church to them. The couple did have a number of other close friends within the church as well, which can be verified by her two daughters.

Bethan's letters home, whether to family or friends, were always full of interesting, funny or descriptive passages in which she shared her and the Doctor's experiences. The letters could almost make a book in themselves! The following, written while in Canada in 1947, is but one example:

> *The wild life up there is interesting—I was amazed to see a <u>humming bird</u> about, not much bigger than a butterfly. What they call robins are tall, lanky, light brown fellows with pale pink shirt fronts—quite unlike our perky little brown balls with red bib ... the chipmunks are sweet—the prettiest little things ... What I am really revelling in is the lovely sense of relaxation and leisure. I shall get too fat to move, but I am thankful for a little while only, of course—for nothing to do and I sit and gaze in amazement at my lily white hands!*

> *The Teacher searched to find just the right words, and*
> *what he wrote was upright and true.*
> ECCLESIASTES 12:10

---

12. See Murray (1990), 101–102.

A postcard sent by Bethan, from Scotland.

An example of Bethan's handwriting.

9

IN JOURNEYINGS OFTEN

For he will command his angels concerning you
to guard you in all your ways.
Psalm 91:11

Worry does not empty tomorrow of its sorrows;
it empties today of its strength.
Corrie Ten Boom

Wales

The Lloyd-Joneses were usually absent from Westminster Chapel from mid-July to mid-September, but only a few weeks of this time were given to a 'proper' holiday, because the Doctor was invariably asked to preach or lecture in many of the places they visited. This pattern continued throughout the 1950s, with the exception of one or two years.

With the great responsibility and pressures which the Doctor carried, it was essential that he and Bethan were able to get away for a complete break each year. The place they enjoyed the most for a summer holiday was Wales, and they never tired of it. Possibly they were experiencing what Welsh people call 'hiraeth': this is a word which it is impossible to translate adequately, but it conveys the idea of deep-hearted longing, especially for one's homeland; yet it is not the same as homesickness. Indeed, for the Doctor and his wife, home was being with each other and, in any event, both were to spend by far the greater part of their lives in London. But perhaps that was why Wales, especially the rural parts of it—away from the hustle and bustle of London—was such a welcome venue for holidays. Not that they were in any way 'nationalistic' in this: Scotland, Ireland, and picturesque parts of England also afforded them great delight. Mrs Lloyd-Jones loved nature and beauty, wherever it was found. The detail of little things would catch her eye and she would be enthralled.

However, although they would not have wanted to have lived permanently in a rural setting, the Doctor and his wife never lost their love of the countryside, especially in Wales. But their love for Wales did not stop with an appreciation of its great scenic beauty: they had a deep concern for the *spiritual* condition of the country as well. This probably explains the Doctor's willingness to preach in his homeland when on holiday, even when this had not always been pre-arranged. There was nothing 'professional' about him as a shepherd of souls and, like Susannah Spurgeon before her, Bethan was willing 'to give up her lamb' during these holiday periods. When staying with their good friends John and Mari Jones at their farm 'Bryn Uchaf' in Llanymawddwy, the Doctor would often preach at the little village chapel they attended.

The Joneses' hospitality acquired something of a legendary status in Wales: over the years they opened their home to ministers, missionaries, and Christian workers, not only from Wales and other parts of the UK, but from all over the world. Bryn Uchaf is situated in a somewhat isolated spot, being reached by the mountain road which winds its way from Dinas Mawddwy up to Bwlch y Groes—a road often traversed by one of the Doctor's spiritual heroes, the great Thomas Charles of Bala. Although their farm was located 'far from the madding crowd', it is no exaggeration to say that John and Mari did not need to see the world because the world, in the form of nationals from different countries, literally came to them. One of the highlights of the many times the Lloyd-Joneses spent there was to gather round the log fire in the evenings, sharing fellowship together with this hospitable couple.

After they had bought their first car, the Lloyd-Joneses were able to visit out-lying districts which had been closed to them hitherto. From Llanymawddwy they were able to travel out each day and enjoy the wonderful countryside of North Wales and visit places of interest. The Doctor never lost his fascination with agricultural life, and one day, while visiting a farm, he and Mrs Lloyd-Jones witnessed something which they had never seen before. Bethan wrote of it to some friends:

> *We had one quite unforgettable day of motoring while we were there—a glorious Summer day with our road lying over magnificent mountain passes & beautiful valleys. We saw the home of Mary Jones of Bible Society fame, & many interesting things including a neat & deft surgical operation by a young farmer, on a sheep which had a cyst pressing on its brain!!* [1]

Wales always had a special place in Bethan's affections. This was, no doubt, because of the numerous friends which she and the Doctor had made during their various visits to the Principality over so many years. This is how she described one of their journeys as they travelled throughout Wales, revisiting some of the families they had known during their marriage:

> *Most of our routes in Wales had many long ago associations for us, too, and we saw people this time that we had not seen for years. It was very pleasant and I enjoyed it all, but it certainly underlined the fact that we are growing old. In one family the children's children are now older than their fathers and mothers when we first knew them.* [2]

---

1. Lloyd-Jones Archive: Bethan Lloyd-Jones to friends.

2. Murray (1990), 280–281.

Mari has spoken of the unselfishness that characterised Mrs Lloyd-Jones. If, when they stayed with her in North Wales, Mari asked her what she would like for supper, Bethan would ask, 'What would you like, Martyn?' Her first thought was never herself, but always her husband. The hospitality which they enjoyed with John and Mari was reciprocated when Mari would stay with them in London— John, of course, had to stay at home to look after the farm. Mari had opportunity to observe them in the midst of their busy schedules and was struck by the love and devotion which they showed to each other. She recalled an incident when the Doctor was about to leave to preach some distance away: it was the warmth of the embrace as he was about to leave which impressed itself on Mari's memory. The Doctor hated to be apart from his wife, even for an hour. If he was away preaching in the week, he would sometimes take an eleven o'clock train just to be back home with her. He often said that he did not enjoy conferences as much as he could have because Bethan was not there, and she equally disliked the days of separation. Those who knew them would say how well suited and at ease they were in one another's company. So to be together on holidays and have time for one another was a great blessing to them.

Mrs Lloyd-Jones wrote of another memorable occasion when they were on holiday at Nanstalwyn, in rural Wales. The Doctor had agreed to preach in a chapel in a nearby isolated location. Bethan remembers Martyn being taken, by the farmer with whom they were staying, in a pony and cart to 'Soar' chapel, while those left behind followed on mountain ponies. It was a nine-mile journey! She wrote of that trek:

> *Now, my pony was the best friend of the pony in the trap, and if the latter broke into a little trot, so did mine—panic on my part, but gleeful amusement on the preacher's! ... It was a glorious day, and the beauty of the scenery indescribable. I shall never forget the sight, looking down at the chapel in the valley, while still some four miles away. Half a dozen or more*

paths led down to it from various directions, and these were all alive with streams of ponies (bearing the congregation!) converging on the little grey-stone jewel in its lush green setting. On arrival, the great stable under the church was soon full to its doors and the rest of the ponies were turned out to the near-by field or enclosure … This morning we counted over seventy ponies. As for the service, never in the whole of Wales would one find a more attentive and appreciative congregation, and the singing was joyous.[3]

They loved these earthy, rural Sundays in the midst of such majestic scenery.

Wherever they holidayed, Mrs Lloyd-Jones was happy with a pattern they established early on in their marriage. And as their children grew older, the children were equally happy with the arrangement. The Doctor would give the mornings to reading, and the rest of the day he was happy to do whatever Bethan—and later, Bethan and the children—wanted. The reason for this arrangement was that it was only during the holiday period that he had sufficient time to do the concentrated reading which big tomes of theology required. This, of course, was a considerable sacrifice on Bethan's part. Her husband had an extraordinarily demanding schedule both at Sandfields and at Westminster, and, in addition to the demands of the pastorate, he was usually away each week preaching a number of times. So to be happy to 'give up her lamb' each morning of their holiday so that he could read really was an act of sacrificial love on her part. Over many years the Doctor was very much a 'pastor of pastors', and he once told a meeting of ministers and gospel workers that 'he read for them'. He would never have been able to have mastered some of the big works which he read and to have been such a help to so many had it not been for Bethan's willingness to go along with his desire to give his holiday mornings to serious study.

3. Murray (1982), 322.

Perhaps as important as the *fact* that she went along with this arrangement was the *spirit* in which she did so. Shortly after Dr Lloyd-Jones' death, Elizabeth gave a lecture on her father and his books—that is, the books which he read. She recalled playing on a beach in Wales during a summer holiday, while her father was sitting bolt upright, dressed in a three-piece suit and hat, reading Emil Brunner's *The Divine Imperative*—a great theological tome! The point which she was at pains to make was that not only her mother but she—and later, her sister—was perfectly happy with this arrangement. It was not that the Doctor was a 'distant' father or one who took no interest in his children. Quite the contrary! Indeed, in that same lecture Elizabeth gave numerous examples of how much he entered into his children's and grandchildren's interests and concerns; rather, his being able to give himself to this serious reading was part of his being equipped to be 'an able minister of the new covenant', and his children gladly accepted this. But they could only do so because their mother was happy with the arrangement and was ungrudging in the way in which she gave him up. How much the evangelical world owes to her for this!

'Trains and boats and planes'

Of course, this pattern of reading in the mornings was just that: a pattern, not a rigid strait-jacket, and there were many exceptions to this. 'Exceptions' clearly became the norm and the order of the day on some of the 'holidays' which they took overseas. If Bethan did not find it a battle to 'give up her lamb', crossing an ocean—be it by boat or plane—was a different matter! One of the Lloyd-Jones' grandsons refers to the highly developed imagination on the Phillips' side of the family,[4] and this was certainly a feature of Bethan's temperament. When allied to a somewhat fearful or anxious disposition, the results could be both terrifying and amusing: terrifying to her but amusing to others, not least to her husband.

---

4. Catherwood (1995), 35.

While travelling by train within Canada, Mrs Lloyd-Jones found herself in a rather startling situation. In writing to her children she explained that, having to retrace their steps on one of their journeys, the Doctor had left two of their cases in the ticket office, which he then intended retrieving during their return journey through that particular railway station, judging that he would have plenty of time to collect them as the train passed through:

> *So on reaching Banff he left Bethan—a solitary passenger in the observation car at the rear of the train—to get the cases. He had scarcely left the carriage when to Mrs Lloyd-Jones' shock she found that it was being uncoupled and then shunted backwards until it came to a stop in a siding, leaving her entirely alone in a lone coach. 'After being turned to stone for some time ... sanity returned and I began to hope that I might yet be hitched on to a now lengthened train and so it turned out to be ... and in the far distance I could see a grinning Dada waving a carton of coffee in each hand'.*[5]

All kinds of locomotion could cause Bethan's imagination to run riot: if she could be alarmed by an incident on a conventional train, how much more might this be the case when the train was electrified! Travelling from Paris to Lausanne on such a train proved to be quite an experience. Writing to friends later, she had this to say:

> *We reached Switzerland upon emerging from a tunnel at Vallorbe, then our train becoming electrified we came hurtling down the mountain side to Lausanne at a terrific rate. I could only murmur to Martyn, 'I hope he knows what he's doing!'* [6]

It would seem that Mrs Lloyd-Jones was on tenterhooks whatever mode of transport she would take. An incident which occurred during her first voyage across the Atlantic provides another striking

---

5. Murray (1990), 282.

6. Archive: Bethan Lloyd-Jones to family from Switzerland.

example of how the same event could be the occasion of both alarm and hilarity. She and Dr Lloyd-Jones had boarded the 'Olympic' at Southampton. That in itself had almost been enough for Bethan, for as she saw the receding figures of her mother and mother-in-law as the ship left the dockside, she began to convince herself that she would never see them, or *terra firma*, again! As the voyage progressed, her fears increased. She imagined all manner of horrors: the very thought that only the ship's frame lay between her and the ocean struck terror into her. She said she could not really enjoy the voyage because her imagination ran riot. It was unfortunate for her, therefore, that she chanced to meet one evening an officer on board. She later recalled their conversation:

> *One night in mid-Atlantic I remember well. It was pitch dark and the thick fog was really a wet drizzle. I was just going into the main lounge when one of the ship's officers began to speak to me. He looked pale and dreary, and, 'Rotten night,' said he. 'Yes, I don't like it,' I replied. He went on, 'It was a night just like this when the "Titanic" went down'. (Oh, help!) 'We were going along like this and then came the alarm and every ship within a reasonable distance of the spot had to go there at once and try to pick up the survivors. We had to change course and we beat our own speed record. But we had been too far away, and were too late to help anyone.' ... I was very thankful when he was called away. Martyn thought it was hilarious that this should have happened to me.[7]*

It must have been something close to a vivid nightmare for Mrs Lloyd-Jones as she sought to keep her fears under control during the long voyage. Her faith certainly had to be exercised during those many days at sea. So much for Bethan's first Atlantic crossing.

Over thirty years after this first voyage, Mrs Lloyd-Jones would make her last visit to the U.S. and fly for the first time in

---

7. Lloyd-Jones (1983), 45–46.

her life. Her imagination was still just as fertile and her fears were still just as real. In a letter to one of the family she described the ordeal of boarding the aircraft, adding that she had found the waiting for the take-off to be just as traumatic—she had felt like a lamb awaiting the slaughter. When the flight was announced and they began to walk the 'endless corridors' to reach the plane, she felt it to be surreal:

> *They were most casual about our passports and money etc. and hardly looked at us. I know now how spies get by! Anyway, at the end of this corridor we had to show our boarding tickets, then, just 2 or 3 steps and there it was—not the gallows!—but an air hostess standing at the door of the plane and in we went and sank into soft, comfortable seats— guess who was in the window seat? Not me! ... Then we had a demonstration of how to put on a life jacket—I still don't know how, because I couldn't hear for the 'machinery' noise going on, air-conditioning or something. Then we were given: your father a little bottle of cologne, another of after-shave, and me perfume! While this was going on we were still at the airport. Then we started moving only to stop again and we did this 3 or 4 times. I, of course, started to think there was something wrong and toyed with the thought that there was still time to get out.*[8]

Suffice it to say, she did not leave the plane, but one can well imagine how relieved Bethan was when she and the Doctor reached their destination!

'What time I am afraid ...'

But it was not only travel—whether by train, boat, or plane—which could fill Bethan's heart with foreboding. During their first visit to North America, an incident occurred which gives us an insight into

---

8. Lloyd-Jones Archive: Bethan Lloyd-Jones to family about first flight.

the anxiety which seemed like a fabric that wove itself around her. She and Martyn stayed at a ranch-type hotel, which they enjoyed very much. But Mrs Lloyd-Jones' imagination got the better of her late one night when, she said:

> *I was roused from a deep sleep of sheer exhaustion and fresh air, to hear loud voices just below my window, and the crunch of wheels on gravel and the snorting and pawing of horses. 'Red Indians' I decided, my heart pounding, and I was just about to wake Martyn up, when I found myself fully awake and recognised the arrival of late visitors! Unlikely? Very, but perfectly true!* [9]

Humorous as these incidents may have proved to her husband, and entertaining as the account of her feelings may be to read today, there is a serious aspect to all of this: though she was fearful, she overcame those fears, and they did not prevent her from accompanying the Doctor on his numerous overseas journeys. The lesson she had learned back in Aberavon—when Martyn was away and, fearing that the house would be washed away by the high tide, she had prayed and experienced an indescribable peace—had not been forgotten. While she might still experience fears—even the fear of taking a tube in London or travelling in a lift—she knew what to do with them. As John Newton memorably expressed it:

> *His love in time past*
> *Forbids me to think*
> *He'll leave me at last*
> *In trouble to sink.* [10]

Bethan's fearful temperament was such that it could easily have rendered her unwilling to travel abroad; her faith enabled her to overcome this. If she may not have been able to say with the

---

9. Lloyd-Jones (1983), 53.

10. John Newton (1725–1807), 'Begone, unbelief'.Christian Hymns 697.

psalmist, 'In God I trust; I will not be afraid',[11] she could certainly say with him, 'When I am afraid, I will trust in you.'[12]

Her trust in the Lord is what kept her through situations which might cause the stoutest heart to quake. While in Cincinnati in 1969, the Lloyd-Joneses witnessed the destruction caused by a tornado which had passed within a mile of them. It was while they were staying at the Regency Hotel that the tornado struck the area. They found themselves amidst 'lashing rain and a howling gale' and were just about hurtled through their hotel doors. There was a path of destruction a quarter of a mile wide. Later they went to see for themselves the havoc that had been wrought. The house in which Bethan had had a meal with a Mrs K. the Tuesday before was certainly affected. She described the scene of destruction:

The house ... had a great plank of wood, from blocks away, hurtle through the roof, through the manhole in the attic floor on to the landing below—& tons of dust and plaster etc. and another plank through the glass of the front door & into the hall & lounge—any one piece could have killed anyone in its way![13]

Bethan appears, however, to have taken it in her stride, but it must have been frightening: the very thought that she could have been in that house when the tornado struck!

From Cincinnati they headed by plane to Pensacola, Florida. They were totally unaware of what awaited them there! They were really looking forward to the trip and arrived to blue sky and sunshine. However, they were surprised to learn that there was great concern over Hurricane 'Camille', which was heading straight towards them. As they arrived at the town there was a lot of activity with many shopkeepers boarding up their properties. Holiday-makers had to

---

11. Psalm 56:4b.

12. Psalm 56:3.

13. Lloyd-Jones Archive: Bethan Lloyd-Jones to the family.

pack up and leave in a hurry. There were also about 100 families who were attending the Conference at which Doctor Lloyd-Jones was to speak and who had been planning to lodge in cottages and bungalows along the beach. They also had to beat a hasty retreat. Mrs Lloyd-Jones shared the sobering news with her family:

Everything you heard was hurricane and it was expected Sunday [evening]. It was hard to believe in view of the blue skies and calm sunshine, but the TV interrupted itself every few minutes to give its distance away and to urge everybody to leave the shores ... about 100 miles away along the coast, where the thing struck, there was death and destruction ... windows smashed and shop goods all over the streets ... the TV team reporting lost everything except their lives and their cameras! ... I certainly would never have believed it ... wooden houses torn to shreds with not a plank standing ... roofs completely blown off and tossed around like cardboard, all wooden sheds etc. reduced to matchwood ... cars overturned and a train blown (or sucked!) off the line and as for the trees, words fail me! Great big, stately trees uprooted, crashed on to houses etc. some sheared off like a hot knife through butter, some broken (like you'd break a stick over your knee) and splintered.[14]

Had Mrs Lloyd-Jones not been able to travel with her husband, it is clear that he would have curtailed his extensive overseas commitments.[15] It is cause for gratitude, therefore, that she was able, if not to remove her fears, to overcome them sufficiently to be able to accompany him. The *spiritual* benefit which God's people experienced in Europe, Africa and especially in the U.S. and Canada—where the Doctor made a number of visits—was incalculable.

14. ibid.

15. Lloyd-Jones (1983), 61.

Diversity in places, people and preaching

But spiritual encouragement is a two-way affair, and Mrs Lloyd-Jones' life was undoubtedly enriched by the fellowship which she enjoyed with Christian brothers and sisters in different parts of the world. Staying with various people from different backgrounds and cultures must have been very tiring and exacting for the Lloyd-Joneses: much of their service for the Lord involved giving of themselves to others; but although tiring, sharing one's life with other believers can be mutually rewarding and enriching. Dr and Mrs Lloyd-Jones had very full and busy meetings with students at International Fellowship of Evangelical Students (IFES) conferences in Europe and America. There was also a trip to South Africa. The descriptions which Bethan sent back to family and friends of their stay there were very informative:

> ... *These reserves are great, rolling, brown-baked hills, rolling away from each side of the road to the distant horizon— nothing but scrub, with an occasional tree and the little 'rondavel', native huts, dotted about in thousands. Someone told us that the ones which have white paint round the doors and windows belong to the Christians (which may mean nothing more than that they no longer observe heathen practices) ... About 200 miles from Durban our good tar road petered out and we were on a dirt road for 100 miles. Words fail to describe the roughness and the dust. To pass anyone else, or to be behind them, was quite blinding and choking and the dust got everywhere, even inside our cases in the boot.*[16]

In the Kruger National Park, which they visited while the Doctor took a break from his preaching and lecturing, Dr and Mrs Lloyd-Jones stayed in some very basic living accommodation. The 'rondavel' in which they lodged had only a trestle table and oil lamp, in addition to their bedding. While staying in this primitive

---

16. Murray (1990), 287.

native dwelling, they had limited amenities. Bethan wrote of their experience from this, as she put it, '<u>very</u> Bush' camp-site:

<u>Satara Camp</u>—<u>Bush (very</u> Bush!) <u>Weds. Aug 20th</u>

We have to wash in a little enamel pan in our hut, with a bucket provided for the slops. In the last camp, and this, Dada could not use his electric razor, so had to buy a safety—for 2/- !! It worked fine this morning, though he had to lather with the Palmolive soap provided, because he refused point blank to pay more for the "craving sheam" than for the razor—he actually said it, just like that; then stopped and said—'What did I say?' & then collapsed helplessly![17]

It was while they were here with Dr and Mrs Bremner, who had accompanied them on this short 'holiday', that the Lloyd-Joneses went 'lion spotting', much to Bethan's dismay. Having watched a pride of lions pass, with blood dripping from their jaws, they then faced the rampage of an elephant—charging straight towards them:

He stopped for a minute and then raised his trunk, half blew, half bellowed at us, and stamped his foot and without any doubt preparing to charge. All this time we were still talking together and nobody listening to anybody—I gave Dr Bremner such a push and said <u>Go</u>—<u>Go on</u>, and I think he thought he had better—so he went!! ... Nothing would ever induce me to put myself in that position again. I kept seeing it all night. Dada loved it all and his only regret is that he didn't have a tape recorder in the car![18]

All such experiences added to the treasure chest of memories which they collected during their journeys, and which enriched their lives together and proved interesting to others.

---

17. Lloyd-Jones Archive: Bethan Lloyd-Jones to family from Africa.
18. ibid.

But as well as a variety of places and people, listening to preaching was an important part of their time away, and there were various preachers whom they had the opportunity to hear. They were able to enjoy fellowship with such well-known evangelical leaders as René Pache, Francis Schaeffer, A.W. Tozer and Billy Graham. Mrs Lloyd-Jones may not have had as theologically constituted a mind as her husband, but she certainly was possessed of true spiritual discernment. This comes through in her observations of Dr Tozer when she was with the Doctor at an IFES conference in Canada in 1957. She expressed her views in a letter sent back home:

> We are having an excellent Conference. One of the very best. Over the weekend there has been quite an influx of visitors and friends of IFES. We had our first hearing of Dr Tozer last night, and I must say that was quite an experience in itself—interesting and refreshing—like nobody else and with a complete lack of the showmanship which spoils so many of the good men this side.[19]

She was less commendatory in what she had to say about aspects of Billy Graham's ministry, though she clearly respected him as a gracious Christian. This is what she wrote in a letter to her family from the Winona Lake Conference Center, Indiana, in 1956:

> Yesterday Billy Graham was here and we had Harringay on a small scale—a replica in every detail—the public invited in and all. I don't think we have any more to say about him than before. No feeling of any true spiritual power, no authority of—the _Word_—only really his own forcefulness. I must also add that I did not have the creepy feeling either. I can't honestly say I felt anything. He is a thoroughly _nice_ person, as are all his team and he said the nicest things about Dada before he started preaching.[20]

---

19. Murray (1990), 285.

20. Lloyd-Jones Archive: Bethan Lloyd-Jones to family from America.

Perhaps a comment needs to be made about this. Towards the end of his life Dr Lloyd-Jones was interviewed by Dr Carl Henry, and the interview was published in *Christianity Today*.[21] During the interview Henry quizzed the Doctor about his attitude to the Graham Crusades. The Doctor made perfectly clear that he regarded Billy Graham as an utterly genuine and sincere man who preached the gospel. He was, however, unhappy with the whole 'invitation system' of evangelism which was espoused by Dr Graham and practised in his Crusades. It seems that it is to this that Mrs Lloyd-Jones was referring in her letter. It seems that what concerned her was the 'razzmatazz' and the danger of the preacher's own personality predominating, rather than the Word. This, it seems, is the reason for the contrast with her assessment of Dr Tozer. Others, especially those who have been soundly converted under Dr Graham's preaching, will, no doubt, query the accuracy of Mrs Lloyd-Jones' assessment of there being no true spiritual power and no authority of the Word in his preaching. Spiritual authority and power may be present on one occasion but not on another. Moreover, there can undoubtedly be a subjective element in all our assessments: there were occasions when some Christians felt cold and untouched by the Doctor's preaching, while others were moved to the very depths of their being. Where all Christians may surely agree and profit from Mrs Lloyd-Jones' assessment of Dr Graham is in the awareness that extraneous things—an emphasis on music, 'hype', etc.—can deflect attention from the authority of God's Word, and that 'personality' may at times have more influence on us than we realise.

'All things are yours'

Holidays and journeys away from home are, of course, not only about things which directly affect our spiritual life. The God of grace is the God of nature, and the God who saves us is the God of

---

21. *Christianity Today*, 8 February 1980.

creation. The predominant problem amongst believers today may well be that we make too much of creation and thus fail to live with the attitude which Paul commended to the Corinthian Christians:

> *What I mean, brothers and [sisters], is that the time is short. From now on those who have wives should live as if they had none; those who mourn, as if they did not; those who are happy, as if they were not; those who buy something, as if it were not theirs to keep; those who use the things of the world, as if not engrossed in them. For this world in its present form is passing away* (1 Cor. 7:29–31).

Some Christians in the past, however, may have failed to hold the teaching of 1 Corinthians 7:29–31 in creative tension with the positive attitude to the creation and its legitimate pleasures which is to be found in 1 Timothy 4:1–5 and 6:17. It is quite clear from Mrs Lloyd-Jones' correspondence with her family that this was not the case with her. It was, as far as she was concerned, perfectly in order to take time out to relax and to enjoy the beauties of nature and the pleasures of sightseeing and of shopping. While staying with friends in Paris, Dr and Mrs Lloyd-Jones were able to have a few relaxing days of sightseeing. Bethan thought it the loveliest city she had ever seen. In a letter to a friend she commented:

> *I think Paris is most beautiful and could have spent more time looking at the lovely shops—of course they shut all day <u>Monday</u>!! Not because of Bank Holiday, but because they always do! Did you ever hear anything so silly?* [22]

In a day and age where many—even Christians—are 'driven' in their approach to life and feel guilty about taking time out, perhaps we too need to be reminded that it is not only legitimate but necessary at times to 'come apart with me and rest awhile'. The vital thing is that we do so 'with him', and thus our Christian life, like our

---

22. Lloyd-Jones Archive: Bethan Lloyd-Jones to family from Paris.

Saviour's robe for which the soldiers cast lots, will have a 'seamless' quality to it. As someone has said, 'If we do not come apart, we will come apart!'

By the time the Doctor died in 1981, he and Mrs Lloyd-Jones had not travelled abroad together for some years, but they still enjoyed visiting John and Mari Jones until the Doctor's health was such that this was no longer possible. It is a measure of how much the beauty of that part of North Wales delighted Mrs Lloyd-Jones and how such fellowship with John and Mari meant so much to her that she continued to spend time there. On occasions she would travel with Hywel Jones, the then Principal of the London Theological Seminary, in the setting up of which the Doctor had been involved in 1977. Hywel would attend the annual Ministers' Conference of the Evangelical Movement of Wales at Bala, which was not far from Llanymawddwy, and he would drive Mrs Lloyd-Jones to Bryn Uchaf and then collect her on his return to London. Distance may have separated Bethan from John and Mari, but their deep friendship and fellowship were such that, as the apostle John did not wish to communicate with his friend Gaius with pen and ink but wished to 'talk ... face to face', so Mrs Lloyd-Jones was willing to make the long journey from London to Llanymawddwy, even in old age, to be able to do the same.

Hywel Jones has commented on Mrs Lloyd-Jones that 'her spiritual life was very natural'. One might add that her natural life was very spiritual. Perhaps one of the most striking examples of this was when she was visiting America. She and the Doctor were travelling by train, and Bethan was mesmerised by the beauty of the landscape. That day she was to learn a very important lesson. They were in a valley and the whole of the hillside opposite was covered with trees. But she saw something which particularly arrested her attention:

I noticed that, right in the middle of the front row of trees, was a different tree. It was a glowing, gold red colour and looked so very beautiful against the dark background. We were getting out at the next stop which we were fast approaching, and I asked one of the men who met us the name of the tree. 'Isn't it beautiful?' said I. 'Yes', he said, 'it does look good there, but it is quite dead, you know. It will stay like that for the summer, but it will be broken to bits by the ice and snow and gales when the hard weather comes—there's no life in it'. I had to believe him. I could see it all. And I thought to myself—that is just like ourselves! We may appear to be wonderful Christians, but it is the 'hard weather' which will test us to see if we have life in us.[23]

> *All things are yours, whether … the world or life or death or the present or the future—all are yours, and you are of Christ, and Christ is of God.*
> 1 CORINTHIANS 3:21b–23

---

23. Lloyd-Jones (1983), 54.

Bethan with Martyn at Bryn Uchaf, 1968.

Bethan with Martyn, crossing the Atlantic.[2]

Bethan outside the Lloyd-Jones' car, with her mother-in-law seated inside.

10

EVER-WIDENING CIRCLES

I waited patiently for the Lord;
he turned to me and heard my cry …
He put a new song in my mouth,
a hymn of praise to our God.
Many will see and fear the Lord
and put their trust in him.
Psalm 40:1, 3

Pray often, for prayer is a shield to the soul, a
sacrifice to God, and a scourge for Satan.
John Bunyan

TRADITION AND 'QUESTIONS OF CONSCIENCE'

Tradition

In many ways Mrs Lloyd-Jones' background was very different from that of her husband: her family had social 'connections', even with a British prime minister, whereas, as one of her grandchildren points out, this 'of course, was not the Lloyd-Jones' style'.[1] But there were

---

1. Catherwood (1995), 31.

other differences, and some of these were to have an influence upon Bethan's spiritual life. Although the Doctor and Bethan were both raised in what was then called the Welsh Calvinistic Methodist Church and, after moving to London, the Lloyd-Joneses attended the same church as Bethan's family, there were considerable differences between the spiritual 'outlook' of the two families. Her family background was evangelical; the Doctor's father, by contrast, had taken up with a kind of theological liberalism whose big emphasis was social justice.

What is interesting, however, is that it was Bethan who, after coming to faith, needed help from her husband in applying and working out her faith in certain areas of life. She had been very much conditioned by the tradition of her church and by her parents' outlook. In particular, her background bred in her a tendency to have something of an over-scrupulous conscience, or what Paul refers to as having a faith which is weak. One of the fascinating things to observe in the Lloyd-Jones' marriage is the way in which the Doctor dealt pastorally with his wife with respect to some of these issues. Since his coming to faith in Christ brought him to spiritual convictions which differed from those of his father and from much of the prevailing religious climate of the time, it was inevitable that, unlike his wife, he had to think things through and apply the first principles of his faith to a range of issues, rather than simply follow what others did.

A question of conscience: The Lord's Day

One area of difference where the Doctor was to help his wife related to the Lord's Day. It is quite clear from his published sermons that the Doctor regarded the Lord's Day as special and had what would be called a 'high view' of it. However, he carefully distinguished this from an over-scrupulous—what some might call a 'legalistic'— attitude to matters of detail. For example, preaching on Romans 14 on a Friday night in the late 1960s, he said, 'I remember in my youth hearing that if any members of the Presbyterian Church of Wales walked on the promenade at Aberystwyth on a Sunday, they would be disciplined before their church'.[2] He cited this as an example of 'over-zealous and strict and rigorous Sabbatarians', who had 'often made the Sabbath a burden and a yoke on the shoulders of Christian people'.[3] Some in Bethan's family had undoubtedly taken this kind of thing to an extreme. Her grandfather, Iorweth Jenkins, would never have his photograph taken as he felt it to be sinful—akin to making an idol. He used to go to bed on a Saturday night in his shoes and socks, so that he would not have to perform unnecessary or extra work on a Sunday!

While Bethan and her parents had a far more common sense approach to things than this it would be true to say that they were 'stricter' than the Doctor in their approach to the Lord's Day. For example, whenever her parents needed to be anywhere early on a Monday morning, they would travel only after midnight in order not to have to journey on a Sunday. Of course, many Christians have had such a view of things: apart from directly 'spiritual' things, only works of 'necessity' or 'mercy' should be undertaken on the Lord's Day. The difference between the Doctor and his wife concerned their view as to what was 'necessary'. His emphasis was more on the positive and on the fact that 'Sabbath was made for man, not man for the Sabbath'; Bethan, on the other hand, tended to think more in terms of what one should not do on the Lord's Day. Her daughter Ann comments that her mother could have been a 'don't do this, don't do that' sort of woman. In this area as in many others, Dr and Mrs Lloyd-Jones complemented one another wonderfully.

Although the Doctor knew more of gospel liberty than his wife and was 'stronger' in faith than she, he was very sensitive to her scruples, which, he believed, were due to her background. A good illustration of their differing views as to what was and was not permissible on the Lord's Day and a fine example of the way in

---

2. Lloyd-Jones (2003), 86.

3. ibid.

which the Doctor respected his wife's conscience is to be seen in a letter dated 10 April 1943, which he wrote to Mr Secrett. At the time of this letter the Lloyd-Joneses were still living in Haslemere, and Mr Secrett had been helping them find a home in London. The relevant parts of the letter read as follows:

> *Dear Mr Secrett,*
> *It is more than likely that I shall see you tomorrow … as I shall tell you tomorrow, my wife's scruples have decided that we shall not view the house tomorrow but wait another opportunity. I think she is right—'whatsoever is not of faith is sin'. 'All things are lawful but all things are not expedient.'*[4]

When one checks the relationship of the date of this letter to the precise day on which it was written in 1943, it becomes clear that this letter was written on a Saturday. Evidently both Mr Secrett and the Doctor were not unhappy about viewing the house the next day—a Sunday—but clearly Mrs Lloyd-Jones' conscience would not allow this. It was not that Martyn and Bethan differed in their belief in the sanctity of the Lord's Day; rather, they differed on details in the area of what this meant in practice. The vital thing to observe is that the Doctor respected his wife's conscience and did nothing to make her violate it. This, of course, is an aspect of true love: curtailing one's own liberty for the sake of another. It is clear from the sermons which he preached on Romans 14, now published as *Romans: Exposition of Chapter 14:1–17: Liberty and Conscience*, that he practised what he preached. In this series of sermons he deals with the objection that if Christians curtail the exercise of their liberty for the sake of those who are 'weak' in faith, then the church will never mature. He points out that the weak in faith need to be taught and instructed. It is, therefore, fascinating to see how Bethan's views underwent something of a modification with respect to certain practical matters on the Lord's Day.

---

4. Murray (1994), 86–87.

On one occasion, during a holiday period, the Lloyd-Joneses were with their children and grandchildren at a sea-side town. The children were told by their parents that they could not go onto the beach because it was a Sunday; they were to do something else. The Doctor was of a different opinion and took the view that the children should be allowed to go on the beach, even though it were a Sunday, because it was such a blisteringly hot day. Bethan agreed with her husband. It was not that she had abandoned her earlier belief with respect to the sanctity of the Lord's Day: the Doctor and his wife were of one mind on this. Rather, with respect to how this worked out in practice, she had clearly come to a different view from that which had been held by those who would have disciplined church members for walking on Aberystwyth promenade on a Sunday. This appears to be an area where the Doctor's approach to things had influenced his wife.

Since the whole question of the use of the Lord's Day has become an area of controversy and disagreement amongst believers in our day, it may be useful to spell out what the Doctor's view was on this, lest the foregoing lead to misunderstanding and misrepresentation of his position. In his sixth sermon on Romans 14, he clearly states that the Sabbath is part of God's moral law, which is not an issue of 'conscience':

> *Sabbath observance is a part of the moral in contradistinction to the ceremonial law. The moral law, the Ten Commandments in particular, has been laid down for all time ... But the moral law has never been abrogated, and is to be perpetually observed. So we must never discuss the keeping of the moral law. It is not to be discussed: it is to be kept; it is to be obeyed; it is to be observed. So I say again that as Sabbath observance is a part of the moral law, it cannot be the matter that the Apostle is dealing with here.*[5]

---

5. Lloyd-Jones (2003), 81.

The Doctor, therefore, held to what is known as a Sabbatarian position. Where he differed from some Sabbatarians—from his wife, for example—was not with respect to the *principle* of Sabbath observance but, rather, how this was to be worked out in certain details. Iain Murray refers to some observations which the Doctor made to the first Westminster Fellowship he attended after returning from his last visit to the U.S. in 1969. He believed that he had seen evidence in one theologically strong denomination in the U.S. of over-attention to detail with respect to Sabbath observance:

> *The danger for people concerned with doctrine was to lose a sense of proportion and to put details before the big general issues. He believed he had seen something of this in the General Assembly of the Orthodox Presbyterian Church, where two days were given to the question of Sabbath observance and the alleged difference between Calvin and the Puritans on that point.*[6]

This, however, did not mean that the Doctor had a lax or cavalier approach to the Lord's Day. On another occasion, when he was still minister in Sandfields, Doctor Lloyd-Jones had been preaching away one Sunday and was returning home by train. It was full of people who had obviously spent the day at the seaside. The following Sunday he took this up in the course of his sermon. The whole context of his remarks indicates that meeting together to worship God on a Sunday was not something which could be isolated from one's total 'world view' and approach to life.[7] In other words, the 'keeping of Sunday special' was not obedience to a discrete commandment, but part of a total life of worship, and of having the Lord at the centre of things. This, of course, is quite different from a legalistic approach, which isolates commands in

---

6. Murray (1990), 618–619.

7. See the quotations from this sermon in Murray (1982), 138.

a mechanical way, and makes them an end in themselves—surely one of the mistakes of the Pharisees.

In other words, Dr Lloyd-Jones was able to differentiate between pleasure seekers—thinking only of themselves, with no thought of God—and his grandchildren being allowed on the beach for part of a Sunday, while on holiday, on a blisteringly hot day. While he and Mrs Lloyd-Jones believed that the Lord's Day was not to be given up to work or even quite innocent pleasures which might be enjoyed on other days, this did not mean that children—especially if they had not yet come to faith and learned the *spiritual* value of the Lord's Day—should not be allowed to enjoy the beauty and comforts of nature on a particularly sweltering day. Authentic holiness makes people more truly human. Principles were not being sacrificed, and Bethan—now having been under the influence of her husband's teaching for many years—wholeheartedly agreed with him on this occasion.

A question of conscience: infant baptism

Bethan's upbringing also influenced her in the area of 'infant baptism'. The Doctor did not believe this to be a scriptural practice. At the time of the birth of their elder daughter, Elizabeth, however, Bethan had not yet come to an experience of salvation. But she was deeply religious at that time and her only thought was doing what she believed to be right. She regarded it as very important that her daughter be baptised. The Doctor believed that his wife's conscience would be far more wounded if he did not allow the ceremony to go ahead, than his conscience would be by Elizabeth's being baptised. Elizabeth, therefore, underwent this ceremony, which was performed by another local minister officiating. It needs to be stressed that Mrs Lloyd-Jones did not have a fully worked out doctrine of infant baptism. She was not like the many Christians who hold to infant baptism as a deeply held conviction which they find in Scripture. By the time Ann was born Bethan had been converted, and she was then governed more by what she believed were the principles of Scripture than by what she had been brought up to believe. Ann was duly dedicated at Sandfields Chapel, but not baptised.

DEVOTIONAL LIFE

Bible reading

Mrs Lloyd-Jones was very disciplined in her reading of Scripture: as well as reading daily with her husband, she had a very structured pattern of reading the Bible for herself. One of her grandchildren has said:

> She would amaze us with the depth of her knowledge, knowing the most obscure passages, and with an ability to remember the most complicated and unpronounceable names.[8]

For most of her married life, Bethan and her husband—separately and on their own—followed the M'Cheyne reading scheme of the Bible:[9] four chapters a day, two from the Old Testament and two from the New. Once the girls professed faith, they also had a family devotional time with their parents. When Doctor Lloyd-Jones was away preaching Bethan would read a passage from the Bible, and she and the girls would say the Lord's Prayer together.

A verse of Scripture that was very dear to her, and which she regularly referred to, is found in Psalm 119:165: 'Great peace have they which love thy law: and nothing shall offend them' (AV). She would quote this verse and call it 'her verse', especially when she or her family faced any difficulties.

Prayer

All who met Bethan Lloyd-Jones testified to her godliness. True godliness grows out of a life spent in communion with God. Mrs Lloyd-Jones did not 'parade' her prayer life, but her Heavenly Father, who saw what was done in secret, rewarded her openly.

---

8. Catherwood (1995), 35.

9. See Appendix 4.

She spent much time in prayer and in contemplation of her Lord and Saviour. She knew Him intimately, and the Lord Jesus Christ became her closest companion. Hywel Jones has commented on the fact that her spiritual life was 'natural'. One is reminded of Andrew Bonar's comment on his close friend Robert Murray M'Cheyne: 'I just can't understand M'Cheyne. Grace seems natural to him'.

Certainly grace never obliterates nature, but sanctifies and purifies it. Something of Bethan's imaginative nature was expressed in the way in which she prayed. Mari Jones remembered well how Bethan would pray aloud in ever—widening circles: she might start by thanking God for her food; then this would lead her on to pray about what to prepare for an evening meal; this would remind her of the butcher—which would lead her on to pray for his salvation. Wherever her thoughts would meander, there she would follow! In this respect there was a similarity between her praying and her letter writing:

> 'Well dearest people, I must end this. I run on like a dog trotting!' [10]

The death of her husband was the hardest thing she had ever had to face in life—she would never be quite the same again. She told Mari Jones that she so missed him, especially the times they spent in prayer and around God's Word. This was one of her greatest losses. No one but the Lord Himself could fill that void!

'Prescience' and second sight?

Mrs Lloyd-Jones' experience of God was more than head knowledge. She knew what it was to walk and talk with Him. She had tried and proved the promises of God. But how far does such intimacy with God extend? In a remarkable sermon on Psalm 25:14, entitled 'The Secret of the Lord', John Kennedy[11]—who was one of the greatest

---

10. Lloyd-Jones Archive: Bethan Lloyd Jones to friends.

11. Kennedy (1979), 201.

preachers in Scotland in the nineteenth century and a good friend of the great C.H. Spurgeon—maintained that this verse taught that God shares with those who truly fear Him 'secrets' which could not be discovered or learned about in any other way. Whatever we make of this understanding of the verse, it is undoubtedly the case that there have been Christians who have possessed a remarkable insight into the secrets of people's hearts as well as having intimations of what will happen in the future. We have already seen that Evan Roberts, who was staying with Mrs Lloyd-Jones' grandfather when she and her brother had been sent to Newcastle Emlyn during the 1904 Welsh revival, knew that a young man who wanted to see him needed only to read Psalm 27:10. Since the young man had been thrown out of his house by his parents the previous night because he had been converted, the verse—'though my father and mother forsake me, the Lord will receive me'—was singularly appropriate to his case. Yet Roberts knew nothing about the young man and nobody had told Roberts about the young man's distressing circumstances.[12] This was something which Bethan remembered all her life.

From time to time Mrs Lloyd-Jones had similar experiences. She almost had a 'second sight'. She would see someone and sense that they were going to die, and very soon afterwards the death would occur. Iain Murray records a remarkable example of this kind of experience. The Doctor had, effectively, been shunned by the medical fraternity in Aberavon. One day, however, as she was coming home from town, Bethan had an intimation that her husband would be called in to advise in the case of a local medical general practitioner. The Doctor dismissed the idea, saying that that was the very thing which could not happen. Bethan stood her

---

12. Something of a similar, though not identical nature, occurred on at least three occasions in Spurgeon's public ministry: see Spurgeon (1973), 59–60.

ground: she *knew* that Martyn was going to be consulted about this problem, and a little later this was exactly what happened.[13]

It is interesting to note that Mrs Lloyd-Jones was somewhat troubled by this kind of thing: she prayed earnestly that she would be delivered from such intimations because they distressed her so much. Usually—unlike the incident referred to in the previous paragraph—they indicated 'some impending disaster', and she found it difficult to cope with this kind of thing. She was concerned that such experiences tended more towards the 'psychic' than being part of any true Christian experience. Interestingly, in an address which the Doctor once gave to a group of ministers in Wales on the 1904 revival, he stated his belief that Evan Roberts—whom he knew personally—had, at times, crossed the line between the 'spiritual' and the 'psychic'.[14] This is an area which can be fraught with danger and which can indeed have harmful consequences for the cause of Christ.[15] On the other hand, some remarkable examples of this

13. Murray (1982), 258–259.

14. The occasion was a message which the Doctor gave in Bala to the annual Ministers' Conference of The Evangelical Movement of Wales on 23 June 1970: 'The Religious Life of Wales at the Turn of the Century'. The late Graham Harrison of Newport, South Wales—one of the ministers who took part in Dr Lloyd-Jones' funeral—made contemporaneous notes of this address, which he later typed up. He gave a copy to my husband in 2004 to help with background material for a paper which my husband was to give that year at the annual Westminster Conference on the subject, 'The Welsh Revival of 1904—Or Was It?' The notes state: 'Certain elements came into the Revival especially with Evan Roberts which were disturbing—his tendency to be mystical—even psychic. He crossed the line partly because of strain and overwork ...' Mr Harrison also typed up notes of a conversation which he had with Dr Lloyd-Jones on 6 May 1974. The notes state: 'When he knew him Evan Roberts was a bit strange and unbalanced. He had crossed the line from the spiritual to the psychic.... When Lloyd-Jones knew him in the '20s and '30s, there was something odd about him... John Phillips'—one of Bethan's uncles—'consulted old Evan Phillips about Evan Roberts (who ... was not doing his school work). Answer:—God is dealing with that young man!'

15. This was undoubtedly the case with Roberts himself, who, it seems,

kind of thing were not unknown amongst the Scottish Covenanters, which, far from working mischief, inspired prayer.[16] Consequently, in answer to her prayers, such experiences left Mrs Lloyd-Jones.

However, there is an interesting sequel to this. Bethan had a friend in the Highlands of Scotland who shared this experience—some might term it a gift—which was identical to her own. They would speak together about this mutual 'experience'. In 1968, this lady had a clear intimation that the Doctor would be leaving Westminster Chapel. She told Bethan, before ever the Doctor knew that he had cancer, 'He will be very ill, but he will live. God will preserve him'.[17]

Money, tithing and 'possessions'

For all of Bethan's family background and connections, and the promising financial security which she and Martyn would have known if they had continued in the medical profession, things obviously turned out very differently as a result of Martyn's becoming a minister of the gospel. A Harley Street consulting physician of Dr Lloyd-Jones' distinction would have easily been able to buy a car. It was, however, only as a result of benefiting from his mother's estate after her death that the Doctor was able to afford one in 1952.[18]

Although they were not rich, as this world deems *rich*, the Lloyd-Joneses were very generous. Like many Christians, the Lloyd-Joneses gave a tenth of their income—a 'tithe'—to the Lord's work. Mrs Lloyd-Jones kept a box in which she set aside this tenth.

---

at times believed himself to be following the leading of the Holy Spirit by being silent in meetings when the people needed to hear the preaching of the Word. On the 'deadening' effect upon prayer which resulted from an opinion of Lachlan Mackenzie, a Scottish preacher of the eighteenth and early nineteenth century who was commonly believed to possess prophetic powers, see Appendix 5.

16. See Appendix 6.

17. As related by Bethan's daughters in conversation with the author.

18. Murray (1990), 280.

She was very keen on bringing her share of whatever she had to God. From the royalties she received for her work in translation, she immediately took from them 'the Lord's portion'. This is what the Lloyd-Joneses regarded as a commitment. Their generosity is to be seen in what they gave away to others. When Gwyn Walters was a travelling secretary with IVF in Wales in 1949–1950—today he would be called a UCCF staff worker—the Doctor thrust a ten shilling note into his hand as a gift: this would be 50 pence today, hardly of any significance. But in those days, ten shillings was a considerable sum of money.

Charity, of course, begins at home, and the Lloyd-Joneses were very generous within the family. Sir Fred Catherwood, speaking shortly after the Doctor's death, commented on the fact that although his father-in-law was always careful with money—he came, after all from Cardiganshire![19]—it was he who provided the deposit for Fred and Elizabeth's first house. Mrs Lloyd-Jones was totally at one with her husband in her generosity within the family. When sending money from America to their family in 1969, Bethan included a note saying:

'We would like the children to have a fiver [£5] each out of this now! For their holiday or whatever.'[20]

Five pounds was a considerable amount of money in those days. At that date there were five grandchildren: £25 was certainly a not inconsiderable sum.

Mrs Lloyd-Jones, although generous, was also frugal— but not miserly. She was very careful with money and did not spend it lightly. She was content not to be modern. For example, Bethan's mother came to live with the Lloyd-Joneses in 1952. Ann remembers her darning the sofa for them—the same sofa which they had

---

19. It is a kind of friendly 'in' joke amongst Welsh people that those who come from Cardiganshire are careful with money. Sir Fred himself alluded to this when referring to the Doctor's generosity.

20. Murray (1994), 220.

had when first married twenty-five years earlier; and at that time Mrs Lloyd-Jones still had the same cooker which she had when she got married. She intended that everything which she bought would last. The Lloyd-Jones' home was 'lived in': it was not a 'museum piece', and Mrs Lloyd-Jones did not set out to impress. But her attitude was the exact opposite of the parsimony displayed by the community of ladies in *Babette's Feast*: she never begrudged others having, and gave gladly to those whom she knew were in need. Whatever the Doctor and Mrs Lloyd-Jones had they willingly shared.

When they were abroad in 1969 we see the Doctor and Bethan's carefulness with money when she sent a letter home to the family with a message for her husband's secretary at Westminster Chapel:

> *N.B. A message for Pam:—(the postage that was to be paid on these forwarded letters is quite shocking and your father feels we must do something about it.) Please tell Pamela to sort out any thing in a business-looking envelope, dividends or anything with the name of a firm, etc. on it and let you have them so that Fred can open them and judge whether they should be sent on to us or whether they will keep. There is a lot of junk in these envelopes and it is madness to pay air-mail on them—the packet that arrived this morning had cost 17/6!!!*[21]

Bethan's concern that Keith (Ann's husband) should not be offended that they were asking Fred (Elizabeth's husband) to sort out their affairs is quite touching, and again demonstrates how wise Mrs Lloyd-Jones was in every situation. She continued her letter:

> *Please Elizabeth explain to Ann that it is not because we think Keith is not a business man that we ask Fred to do this, but because a lot of this stuff is from Warburg, the firm that is from now on going to look after all our affairs and whom Fred knows and introduced us to and whom Fred can contact and*

---

21. Lloyd-Jones Archive: Bethan Lloyd-Jones to family from America.

speak to if any question should arise. K & A will understand this, so please tell them.[22]

The Lloyd-Joneses were very fortunate in having such a capable son-in-law. Sir Fred Catherwood was able to advise them on various investments they were able to make of monies they received when their respective parents died, and then later, of the royalties they received for their books—particularly those of Dr Lloyd-Jones. It would seem that it was Bethan who took charge of the accounts in this respect. She had quite a number of books filled with her financial records. Bethan was not only astute with 'folk' but also with 'figures'!

A gift

When Elizabeth and Ann were asked what they felt was their mother's greatest gift, they both replied, 'Wisdom'. There are many examples that could be cited of this 'heavenly' wisdom which she possessed, but the following extract may give us some idea of that gift with which Bethan Lloyd-Jones was endowed. She needed no time to think or consider her response to a problem that had taxed a particular young woman for a considerable time:

After a number of years struggling with being single, as a woman in my late twenties/early thirties, I faced a dilemma. A male friend of mine had become convinced that God was directing us to begin a relationship that would in due time lead to marriage. He sent letters outlining his conviction as well as giving me books in which he had underlined passages backing up the general position he was taking in an attempt to encourage me to do the same. He spoke to my parents, sharing his feelings and asking for their help and advice. I was confused. I did not want to go against what might be the will of God, but I was not sure how I felt towards him. I had been

---

22. ibid.

single for a number of years and time was moving on. Perhaps this man was God's provision for me. How could I be sure?

The matter was brought to a swift and clear conclusion by a visit from Mrs Lloyd-Jones. Her husband was preaching in the locality and knowing my parents, she came to our home for tea. During her time with us Mrs Lloyd-Jones asked how I was, and in response, my mother told her of my current dilemma. The way she dealt with the issue for me was both wise and practical. She did not give me an extensive exposition of the principles of God's guidance or the theology of marriage: she simply asked me one practical question that crystallised what I needed to see to bring this matter to a close.

'Would you be happy to see his face next to you on the pillow when you wake in the morning?'

When I replied, 'No', she simply said, 'Well there's your answer then!'

There was no more need of discussion. We got married some time later, but as a result of Mrs Lloyd-Jones advice, it was not to each other! [23]

There was another story of a married woman, but on this occasion Mrs Lloyd-Jones was left feeling acutely embarrassed: in fact, up until this time it was the only really awkward situation in which she found herself as a minister's wife. This particular woman was a missionary on furlough—what is today known as 'home assignment'—and she had been asked to speak about the work she and her husband were involved in overseas. She had not really gauged the Ladies' Meeting aright, and was unwise—to say the least—in majoring less upon the work which they were doing abroad and more upon the painful parting from their children:

... she gave a vivid description of her husband and herself bidding good-bye to their—three or four—young children, as

---

23. A correspondent to the author about Mrs Lloyd-Jones' wisdom.

they left for the foreign field. She was graphic, and feeling that she had a sympathetic audience, she really gave a heart-rending picture of the farewell scene, the heart-broken children sobbing and crying with arms outstretched for 'Mummy, Mummy'... the result was not what she expected ... There was a stony, not to say belligerent, disapproval on every face ... I could hear mutterings: 'Better for her if she'd stayed with those children.' 'Why have them if you're not going to look after them?' 'Poor kids, what effect will it have on them?', etc., etc.[24]

Suffice it to say that the missionary did not produce the effect for which she had looked: she produced rather 'a stony, not to say belligerent, disapproval on every face and the meeting ended in a chill that could be felt'. Bethan remembered 'the acute embarrassment of the situation'. The result: silence! Yes, wisdom can sometimes demand just that—silence.

But the wisdom that comes from heaven is first of all pure; then peace-loving, considerate, submissive, full of mercy and good fruit, impartial and sincere.
James 3:17

---

24. Lloyd-Jones (1983), 19.

Bethan after the death of her husband,
at the Welsh Aberystwyth Conference with Mari Jones.

11

A TIME TO PUT ONE'S FEET UP?

The righteous will flourish like a palm tree ...,
planted in the house of the Lord ... .
They will still bear fruit in old age,
they will stay fresh and green,
proclaiming, 'The Lord is upright;
he is my Rock.'
Psalm 92:12–15a

Teach me to treat all that comes to me with peace of soul
and with firm conviction that You will govern all.
Elisabeth Elliott

Different marching orders

In 1968 Dr Lloyd-Jones retired as minister of Westminster Chapel. Having first joined Dr Campbell Morgan in 1938, becoming associate minister with him in 1939 and then sole minister in 1943, it was indeed the end of an era. It would not be an over-statement to say that it was not easy for the church to come to terms with the fact that something of a marathon ministry had come to an end. But while it is undoubtedly true that the loss of the Doctor to the church left something of a huge gap, it was no less the case that the loss of Mrs Lloyd-Jones was also keenly felt by the members and congregation of Westminster Chapel. For many years she had been a confidante and counsellor to numerous people in the church, and had led the ladies' Bible class: and now she, like her husband, would no longer be with them. It was truly a double blow.

It all happened so unexpectedly. The first Sunday of March 1968 found Mrs Lloyd-Jones phoning Edwin King, who was Dr Lloyd-Jones' assistant, to inform him that he would be needed that day to preach at Westminster. Although the Doctor had been feeling somewhat unwell through the previous week, he had put this down to the after-effects of influenza. He preached on the first Friday evening in March the three-hundred-and-seventy-second sermon in his Romans series, on the word 'peace' in Romans 14:17. It was a singularly appropriate word, for the peace of God was something which both he and Mrs Lloyd-Jones would need and experience over the next weeks and months. The sermon that Friday night would prove to be the last which he would preach as minister of Westminster Chapel. Sometime between the Friday night and the Sunday morning he realised that there was something seriously wrong with him. By the Thursday of that week he had undergone surgery to remove a blockage in his colon caused by cancer. While many prayers from all over the world went up to the throne of grace for his recovery, prayer was also offered for Mrs Lloyd-Jones. One of the letters she received during this time not only expressed sympathy for her but also testified to what she meant to so many people:

> *For you to just have to watch and wait is a tremendous strain, but to know so many folk are standing by will help ... you are always the first to uphold and strengthen others and we would long to help you.*[1]

---

1. Lloyd-Jones Archive: Member at Westminster Chapel to Mrs Lloyd-Jones.

Although Bethan had been very apprehensive about the surgery which her husband was to undergo, he believed that he had an assurance from God that it would be successful. Yet he also believed that this was the 'cue' for him to lay down the work at Westminster and to concentrate on 'writing up' his sermons for publication and to give help to churches around the country by preaching for them. Leaving the chapel where, unobtrusively and behind the scenes, she had served the Lord and His people so well for so many years was as difficult for Bethan as it was for the Doctor, whose work there had been so much more prominent. She had greatly enjoyed the sense of belonging to the church family there such that when she knew that she would be leaving, she said, 'I'm going to find it so difficult because I feel as though my whole life has been spent there'.

But if she was to find it difficult, the people in the church were to find it to be no less so for them. Many letters expressing appreciation for the Doctor's remarkable ministry were received at that time. Significantly, a number of them also testified to all that Mrs Lloyd-Jones had meant to so many. The following extract from a letter addressed to them both shows how deep was that bond between the people and Bethan:

> My prayer, each day, has always been that God would bless our beloved minister and his dear wife—and my prayer will be the same until I die ... I love you and Mrs Lloyd-Jones better than anyone in this world ... I know you will realise how sad we all are to know that the Doctor has given up his ministry at Westminster, but we are equally sad that this means we shall be losing you too. You have been such a kind adviser to us, so forbearing with all of us, and we shall miss you terribly.[2]

Although she would never have said—or thought—it herself, such service of the Lord's people would have been costly and demanding,

---

2. ibid.

in more ways than one. One letter which she received displays insight into what this must have involved:

> *For you, I cannot help feel change will not be easy. I know that the strain of listening to and advising all and sundry, all these years, has been very great physically and mentally, but I do hope it has brought some satisfaction in the knowledge that many rise up and call you 'Blessed.' ... I shall miss you very much.*[3]

For many people, retirement is a time to put one's feet up, to travel, to enjoy hobbies which one may have had little time for during working years and to spend more time with family. Certainly some of these things were true for Mrs Lloyd-Jones, now that her husband had retired from the pastorate at Westminster Chapel. Ever since their younger daughter Ann had married in 1965 Bethan and Martyn had lived in the same home as Ann and her husband Keith: the Lloyd-Joneses lived in the ground floor flat, and the Desmonds on the first floor. Ann and Keith's first child, Elizabeth, was born in 1968 and her sister, Rhiannon, was born two years later. The Desmond family circle was completed in 1971 with the birth of the youngest child, Adam. As they grew, the Desmond children were often in their grandparents' part of the house, and the bond between grandchildren and grandparents was very close indeed.

Although the Lloyd-Jones' home was in Ealing, it was in the home of their elder daughter, Elizabeth, in Balsham, Cambridgeshire, that the Doctor did much of the work on his manuscripts for his books. Dr and Mrs Lloyd-Jones were as devoted to Fred and Elizabeth's children as they were to Keith and Ann's: the Catherwood grandchildren arrived a lot earlier than the Desmond grandchildren.

While at the Catherwoods' home Mrs Lloyd-Jones loved to play croquet, and she was quite adept at it, having had considerable

---

3. ibid.

experience playing it when a young woman at her parents' home in Harrow. Christopher and his grandfather were not a match, it seems, for his mother and grandmother! (Was this reminiscent of the fact that, as a young lady, Bethan had been a far more accomplished tennis player than the man she was to marry? In those far-off days of the early twentieth century, tennis and croquet had been joined together: Wimbledon, after all, is the home of the All England Lawn Tennis and Croquet Club.)

There was also certainly time to travel after the Doctor retired. It was in the first full year of his retirement that he and Mrs Lloyd-Jones made their final visit to the U.S., this time for an extended stay. But it would be wrong to think of these retirement years as an endless round of time with family, playing croquet, and travelling. Quite the contrary! It was during their last trip to the U.S. in 1969 that, in addition to giving the lectures at Westminster Seminary—which would subsequently be published as *Preaching and Preachers*—the Doctor began the arduous work of editing his sermons on Romans for publication, and Mrs Lloyd-Jones helped in the preparation of the first volume of the series, which was published in 1970.

Back in the UK, throughout his retirement the Doctor was usually preaching away each Sunday—frequently on the Saturday as well, at the same place—and continued to preach in different parts of the country in the middle of the week. Sometimes Mrs Lloyd-Jones would accompany him on these visits, but frequently this would not be so. In addition to his preaching the Doctor still chaired the Westminster Fellowship of Ministers, which met each month at Westminster Chapel, and the Puritan Conference (later to become the Westminster Conference), which met over two days each December and at which he always gave the closing address. Unless illness prevented him he continued to attend the Ministers' Conference of the Evangelical Movement of Wales held each June in Bala—not the most accessible part of Wales—chairing the discussion sessions and delivering the closing message, as well as day conferences organised by 'the Movement' at its base in South Wales. Furthermore, he continued his involvement with The Evangelical Library, of which he was the president. In addition to these many commitments he constantly gave freely of his time to ministers with pastoral or church problems, frequently spending considerable periods of time on the phone. What all of this means, of course, is that retirement for the Doctor was hardly the life of leisure which it is for many people, and so in old age Mrs Lloyd-Jones was still 'giving up her lamb': she was still 'sharing him' with others, still supporting him in his service for the Lord, still being sacrificial in her service of God and of others. If it is true that as we grow older we become more like we are, then this was pre-eminently the case with Mrs Lloyd-Jones.

But it was not only the Doctor who was busy in retirement; it was during these years that his wife proved her skills as a translator. The first book which she translated from Welsh into English was a spiritual classic by the great eighteenth-century hymn writer, poet and preacher, William Williams—or, as he is more frequently alluded to in Wales, Williams, Pantycelyn or simply Pantycelyn. The Doctor wrote the Introduction to the translation, and in it he tells us, 'I encouraged my wife to translate it'. Mrs Lloyd-Jones was fascinated by words: we saw in an earlier chapter that she loved to discover the etymology or origin of words, and Christopher tells us in *The Family Portrait* that she and his mother reigned supreme at Scrabble within the family, 'since they … knew words of which none of us had ever heard!'[4] Her love of poetry also bespoke an interest in language and in the different ways that it can be used, while her gift as a letter writer reveals a woman who, like the wise Teacher of Ecclesiastes, knew 'just the right words'. One can well understand, therefore, why the Doctor encouraged his wife to translate this work. Just as he had been concerned that she continue to use her mind during the war years when she was with Elizabeth

___
4. Catherwood (1995), 181.

and Ann in Llanelli and without a maid, so now in retirement he had the same concern for her. If she supported her husband in his great work, it was no less the case that he saw her as a person in her own right, possessed of gifts which he did not have, and that she should be encouraged to use them for the glory of God.

Good translation work requires a number of skills, but it requires something more than just skill: while a person must have a thorough grasp of both the languages—the language from which one is translating and the language into which one translates— there is also the need for an artistic flair, something which cannot really be taught. When the great Bible translator William Tyndale 'invented' the word 'scapegoat' and coined the phrase 'by the skin of their teeth', he demonstrated that, while he may have possessed a remarkable grasp of Hebrew and Greek, he had a rare 'feel' for the English language and how to use it to maximum effect. Mrs Lloyd-Jones may not have been a twentieth-century Tyndale, but the very title which she gave to Pantycelyn's book demonstrated that she, too, had a feel for the right words. A literal rendering of the original Welsh title would be 'A Door into the Society Meetings', which would hardly have conveyed much to readers in the 1970s! The translation which she came up with was not only faithful to the meaning of the Welsh but also communicated precisely what the book was about: *The Experience Meeting*. The sub-title expanded upon this: *An Introduction to the Welsh Societies of the Evangelical Awakening*. The *seiat* or 'society meeting' of the Welsh Calvinistic Methodists was precisely that: it was a small group meeting where members would be encouraged to share their spiritual experiences. It was neither a Bible study nor a doctrine study, but an opportunity for believers to share their failures and victories, their barrenness and blessings, and, in a phrase, to open their hearts to one another. Such a meeting, of course, could be fraught with dangers: it could lead to spiritual exhibitionism, to spiritual 'navel gazing' and indiscretion in what was being talked about, as well as degenerate into downright gossip. It was at this point that Pantycelyn revealed something of his spiritual 'genius': for the book is really a guide to the blessings of holding such meetings, as well as about the possible dangers and problems which could arise, and how such meetings should be conducted.

It is not without significance that the 1970s was a decade when, in certain Christian circles, there was great emphasis being placed upon spiritual experience and spiritual experiences, such an emphasis frequently being uncoupled from the biblical framework and categories within which true spiritual experience is to be found. In his introduction to the book Dr Lloyd-Jones referred to this trend and phenomenon as something which was impoverishing Christians and which was inimical to true spirituality. When one considers the spiritual context in which Mrs Lloyd-Jones translated this work, one can appreciate just how 'in tune' she was with what was happening, and how appropriate was the translation which she had given. The rest of the book does not disappoint: it reads easily.

More translations were to follow, this time of a living author. Mari Jones, whom we have already met and who, with her husband, was a close friend of the Lloyd-Joneses, had written a book of 'parables' drawn from farm life. The year after *The Experience Meeting* was published, a translation by Mrs Lloyd-Jones of an earlier Welsh publication by Mari appeared under the title *In the Shadow of Aran*.[5] (Aran is a mountain in North Wales, near to where John and Mari lived.) Dr Douglas Johnson, who for many years had been the General Secretary of the IVF (now UCCF) and who, himself a medical doctor, had worked closely with Dr Lloyd-Jones in IVF and in the Christian Medical Fellowship, was very impressed with the book. He wrote to Mrs Lloyd-Jones to express gratitude and to urge her to continue in this translation work.

Dear Mrs Ll-J, 18 Nov. /78
I've just received from Evang. Movement of Wales—'In the Shadow of Aran.' This is first class stuff—just the thing for

5. See Jones (1976).

rural areas (we've sheep all round here!). We'll get a copy off to Newfoundland.

This form of Gospel is the way the Bible itself approaches— real people pursued by a real saving God in the context of His redeeming providence.

We land whatever unobtrusively can be got into the hands of the retired folk, who spend a great deal of the week reading.

(To several it has opened up a new world, they did not know existed!)

Please let us know of anything of real quality like this, which rings true.

Yours in Christ, D.J.[6]

But this was not the end of the letter. In the bottom left-hand corner, Johnson—or D.J., as he was affectionately known to many— had scribbled: 'Translate like fury if you've got more of this sort of thing!!!!' She did have 'more of this sort of thing'! She was later to translate other books of parables from farm life by Mari Jones: *In the Shelter of the Fold* and *When Swallows Return.*[7]

In fact, her translation work had begun some years earlier: or, to be more precise, her 'approving' of translation. In 1969, a Mrs Williams requested Mrs Lloyd-Jones to translate a beautiful Welsh hymn for her,[8] but before she could attempt it, the Doctor had set about the task. She wrote to the lady saying that she thought the Doctor's rendering of it to be as close to the original as one could hope for in translating from one language to another, which, she explained, was doubly difficult in verse. Evidently the Doctor had either sought her approval of it or she had considered the translation and concluded that it could not be improved upon. When replying to Mrs Williams, Bethan stressed that it had been no trouble to attend to the matter:

6. Lloyd-Jones Archive: Douglas Johnson to Bethan Lloyd-Jones.

7. See Jones (1979) and (1992).

8. See Appendix 7.

This has been no 'trouble' but a great pleasure, and we both hope it is what you want.[9]

Nothing, it seems, was too great or too small to undertake to be of service to God's people.

End of days

The Doctor's retirement years had truly been fulfilling and happy ones for him and his wife. They had been married for over forty-one years when he retired, and they were to have just over another thirteen years of blissfully happy married life together. On 1 March 1981—St David's Day, the day of the Welsh patron saint, and exactly thirteen years to the day that the Doctor had preached his last sermon as minister of Westminster Chapel—their fifty-four years of married life came to an end. Even the greatest Christians have to die, and their loved ones are left with the pain of loss. His death was not sudden but the result of cancer. The surgery he had undergone in 1968 to remove the blockage in his colon had been successful, and he was able to enjoy a very active retirement. In 1976 he had had his prostate gland removed, but continued to fulfil his many engagements until, in 1979, there were, in Iain Murray's words, 'disturbing symptoms'. By the beginning of 1980 the recurrence of cancer meant that most of his public ministry was over.

Iain Murray refers to the fact that the Doctor was glad that he had time to prepare for his death and to meditate upon it. But if he was living with the realisation that he was a dying man and that his time was short, it was no less the case that Mrs Lloyd-Jones must have been aware of this and was having to cope with the prospect of the loss of her husband and all that this would mean for her. At the end of his great Sermon on the Mount Jesus refers to the trials of life which come to all: the wind and the rains beating against the little house of our lives, and the floods rising against them. These are the real tests of what our Christian faith has been: whether real

---

9. Lloyd-Jones Archive: Bethan Lloyd-Jones to Mrs Williams.

and built upon rock, or a pretence which, while appearing to the casual observer to be very impressive, lacks a good foundation and collapses under the tests of life. For over fifty years Mrs Lloyd-Jones' faith had been lived out in the context of being a support to a man of God who, in evangelical circles as well as further beyond, was something of a household name. How would she respond to the very different role of caring for a dying man and subsequent widowhood? The answer can be summed up in one word: magnificently.

The last visit to Wales which the Lloyd-Joneses made together illustrates the 'quiet, calm confidence' which Mrs Lloyd-Jones displayed at this time. It was in Aberystwyth that Dr Lloyd-Jones was to preach his last message in Wales on 14 May 1980. It was a beautiful summer's evening and, after the meeting was over, people mingled in the street outside and spoke with the Doctor and his wife. Iain Murray quotes Geoff Thomas' memory of that night: '… there was a common feeling of joy and thankfulness'. 'Joy and thankfulness': these were the feelings which predominated, not gloom and sadness. No doubt the truth of 'her verse', Psalm 119:165, was continuing to keep and uphold Mrs Lloyd-Jones at this time: 'Great peace have they which love thy law: and nothing shall offend them' (AV).

Thankfulness to God for his wife and for all that she had been and meant to him was something which the Doctor expressed at this time. Bethan continued to mean so much to her husband as, together with Ann and Elizabeth, she cared for him throughout the months of his final illness. The Doctor and his wife had complemented each other perfectly. Since he had been the one who had made the decisions and since she, 'the weaker vessel', was the one who would be left, it was inevitable that the Doctor would be concerned as to how she would be after his days. Iain Murray records Dr Lloyd-Jones' words at this time:

When this illness came, because of my being the one who had made the decisions I was a bit troubled about Bethan and the children after I have gone and tended to worry as to what would happen to them. I have been delivered from it completely. I know that God can care for them much better than I can and that no longer troubles me at all.[10]

Evidence of the kindly care of her Heavenly Father for her was to be experienced by Bethan the night before her husband died. The Doctor had been in his sitting-room chair, but by bedtime he was unconscious. Bethan and her daughter Ann were faced with the difficulty of how to get him into bed. The need was met when two ambulance men responded to Mrs Lloyd-Jones' call for help, and they dealt with the problem for her by carrying him to bed. To the last Bethan was with her husband: on coming round, he drank a cup of tea which she had made for him and then he fell into sleep. By the time that Bethan awoke the next morning, Dr Lloyd-Jones had 'fallen asleep in Jesus', and Bethan and her family were left to mourn 'but not as those without hope'.

The 'great peace' which belongs to those 'who love thy law' was certainly with Bethan on the day of her husband's funeral. Sulwyn Jones, a Welsh pastor who, like so many of his generation, had been greatly helped by the Doctor over the years, commented later in the day to one who had been unable to be present at the funeral on the calmness of everything. Light rain was falling at the graveside, and Sulwyn was standing quite close to Mrs Lloyd-Jones. He noticed that she was unprotected from the rain and so passed her his umbrella. She, in turn, urged him to join her under it. How typical of her! Even at such a sad moment, she was not self-absorbed, not so taken up with her own grief that she was not able to see the needs of others—needs, which in comparison with her own at that point, were indeed trivial. But such was the measure of the woman. Sulwyn Jones was struck by the fact that, at such a time of loss, Mrs Lloyd-Jones was still concerned about others in such an ordinary, non-ostentatious way. She even sought him out,

---

10. Murray (1990), 746.

personally, to return the umbrella after the funeral service was over. Indeed, 'great peace have they which love thy law: and nothing will offend them'. It truly was 'her verse'.

Alone—but not alone

It is one thing to experience peace and calm on the day of the funeral of someone who has gone to be with the Lord; it is a very different thing in the ensuing weeks, months, and years to get up each day and continue with life, when one who has been so much part of that life is no longer around. But this is something which, by the grace of God, Bethan Lloyd-Jones did, and did to the glory of God.

There are always things to attend to in the days and weeks after a funeral. Many people had sent cards and letters of condolence to Mrs Lloyd-Jones at the time of the Doctor's death, and to many of these she wrote to express her appreciation of their concern for her. Thankfulness is a major theme of these letters. In fact, some who owed a great deal to the Doctor and, indirectly, a great deal to his wife, continued to express their gratitude to her on the anniversary of her husband's death. The Westminster Fellowship was a fellowship of ministers who met monthly at Westminster Chapel under the chairmanship of the Doctor. Men received so much help from these gatherings that they would travel many miles to be present at them, and the number of men attending ran into the hundreds. Such was the closeness of the bond which was forged between the Doctor and the men who gathered that some nicknamed it 'the Westminster Confession'—this being a reference not to the seventeenth-century statement of faith which goes by that name but, rather, to the fact that many would pour out their hearts privately to the Doctor during the lunch break. Each year, on the anniversary of his death, the Fellowship sent flowers to Mrs Lloyd-Jones. Her letters back to the secretary of the Fellowship are filled with gratitude for the thoughtfulness and concern which these gifts expressed.

March 7th 1983.

My dear friends,

This letter was intended to reach you at Westminster Chapel this very morning, while all the 'Westminster Fellowship' are all gathered together, and I am really distressed that my good intentions have been frustrated—and chiefly through my own stupidity.

I do hope that the next meeting will not be too late to bring my thanks and so deep appreciation for your act of loving remembrance … I will never forget—the flowers were most beautiful and still are a whole week later … I don't know how to find words to tell you what they did for me. They lifted me right out of a sad grey 'heartache', and filled me with joy and a deep thankfulness. I was very moved, and I thank you all, with all my heart.

May the Lord bless each one of you,

> *Yours, with a very grateful heart,*
> *Bethan Lloyd-Jones.*[11]

The heartache to which she refers was to remain. The following year she wrote as follows:

I remember Martyn once preaching on the text—'Take with you words …' & I simply long for the words which would give you, and all the 'Westminster Fellowship', some idea of my feelings when I received your most beautiful flowers at the door yesterday morning. It was a lovely way of letting me know that you remembered, and my heart was overflowing with love and thankfulness.

Time is very strange—sometimes I think, 3 years and it's like 'yesterday', and at other times, 'only 3 years, and it seems like a life time' and my loss is as real as ever.

---

11. Bethan Lloyd-Jones to the Westminster Fellowship. Kindly lent by Rev. Basil Howlett.

> *But God is very kind, & I am sure that it's only by His grace that we can bear sorrow without bitterness ...* [12]

This extract is interesting because although she had grown up in the Edwardian era—a much more 'formal' period than the 1980s—it is clear that she was quite ready to open her heart and her feelings to these servants of God whom she loved 'in Christ'.[13]

If God's grace enabled her not to give way to feelings of bitterness, the tendency to feel sorry for oneself may have been more difficult to deal with. Thus, in the last of her surviving letters to the Fellowship, she wrote as follows:

> *I was rather under the weather physically and mentally, & losing Martyn was no easier after 8 years! In fact, there is no doubt that I was full of self-pity when I should be full of thanksgiving! Then, in came Elizabeth, with a huge armful of flowers—from you my faithful friends, & your loving sympathy brought me to my senses, & my heart was warmed, and I began to feel better from that moment—'The Lord is rich and merciful', yes, and 'The Lord is <u>very kind</u>!'* [14]

Self-pity may be difficult to deal with, but deal with it she did, and it is deeply instructive to see how she did so. Just as Paul expressed gratitude to the Philippians for their generosity to him, so she was profoundly grateful to Christian brothers for their act of fellowship and sympathy in remembering her in her loss. But she saw beyond the horizontal level, vital though that is, to the vertical dimension: it was the Lord who was rich and merciful, it was the Lord who was very kind, and He was showing that kindness to her through His people.

---

12. ibid.

13. There seems to be an interesting contrast between Mrs Lloyd-Jones and the Doctor with respect to their approach to being 'formal' and 'reserved', or 'informal' and 'open': on this, see Appendix 8.

14. Bethan Lloyd-Jones to the Westminster Fellowship. Kindly lent by Rev. Basil Howlett.

There is, of course, a fine line between the sadness and sorrow which is part of our being human and that which is the result of our sin or yielding to temptation. Jesus experienced sorrow and was sinless. A 'holiness' which makes us less than truly human is not authentic, biblical holiness. There *is* a time to mourn. Furthermore, the Christian life has to be lived out on a daily basis, and triumphing over feelings of self-pity one day does not mean that such feelings will not have to be dealt with the next day.

It was not just the Westminster Fellowship, with whom Bethan's husband had been associated, but also the people of Westminster Chapel—and, in particular, Dr R.T. Kendall, the minister of the Chapel—who showed considerable kindness to Bethan. After Doctor Lloyd-Jones died, Dr Kendall was a regular visitor to the home: he was kindness and consideration itself. As Kendall would take her hand in his, Mrs Lloyd-Jones would say, almost mischievously: 'You are such a flirt!' Ann said her mother greatly appreciated these visits.

Sometimes, if one of her daughters took her out for a coffee, they might see their mother looking wistfully at an elderly couple sitting at a table, perhaps in the corner of the café. When asked about this, she would say, 'It makes me feel so jealous for the same again'. To be jealous *of* people is sinful; to be jealous *for* 'the same again' was surely being human, not being sinfully human. The adjustment to no longer being the most important person in someone else's life takes time.

In her old age Mrs Lloyd-Jones found it more and more difficult to shop for her own clothes. Her husband had always encouraged her to dress well, and had taken an interest in whatever she wore. In fact, he had quite an influence over the things she bought. Bethan liked clothes but was not very fashion conscious. She never wore flat heels as Martyn thought she looked more attractive wearing heeled shoes: this she did all her life. As she grew older, it was necessary for Ann to buy her mother's clothes: she would take them home from the shop to check that they were suitable, and if not, would return them in due time. When Ann had been shopping for her, Bethan would ask, 'What have you got for me today, dear?' Ann said her mother was very easy to please and would have looked beautiful if she had worn a sack!

Something which Bethan was unable to do after the Doctor died was to listen to his voice on tape or, later, on CD. A younger woman, who had never heard Doctor Lloyd-Jones preach when he had been alive but who had been listening to one of the Doctor's sermons and had found it greatly beneficial, thought it might encourage Mrs Lloyd-Jones if she in turn listened to the same message. She therefore suggested that Mrs Lloyd-Jones listen to the sermon too. With great sadness Bethan simply said, 'Oh I couldn't do that—no, I just couldn't listen to his voice'.

What a blessing Mrs Lloyd-Jones' family proved to be to her through the years of her widowhood! Her time was divided between being with her daughter Ann—where they both had their separate flats in the same house—and with Elizabeth in Cambridge. Elizabeth's husband, Sir Fred Catherwood, has written of her during this period:

> Elizabeth's mother, Bethan Lloyd-Jones, lived with us and with her other daughter, Ann, until she died at the age of ninety-two, in full possession of her faculties and able, to the last, to tell us what to do. She was a great character ... She retained her beauty and dignity to the end ... She looked after her own mother (known as Mamgu Bach) until she died in her nineties, and it was inconceivable that we would not keep her with us in the ten years while she was herself a widow. It was sometimes difficult juggling with diaries, but her company was its own reward.[15]

Bethan once described herself, playfully, as a:

> ... 'parcel'—being picked up at Ealing, set down at Balsham, only to be transported back again. In one full calendar year,

---

15. Catherwood, Sir F. (1996), 209.

*she counted that she had spent the identical number of days
with each of her devoted daughters, Elizabeth and Ann.*[16]

When she stayed at Balsham with the Catherwoods, Mrs Lloyd-Jones
would insist on locking her bedroom door, *afraid* someone could
get in, although it posed a bigger problem for her daughter if *she*
needed to 'get in', should her mother have fallen, or were she to be
taken ill during the night. Her anxious temperament never left her:
it remained life-long! She often surmised that she—and sometimes
others—had far worse illnesses than their symptoms indicated.
She regularly 'imagined' the worst. It was her way of coping. She
enjoyed the relief when she was proved wrong! Ann remembers a
conversation she overheard her mother having with someone on the
phone. 'No, Ann hasn't got breast cancer … it was something else'.

Bethan Lloyd-Jones was not only blessed with having a loving
and caring family; she also had good friends with whom she loved
to spend time. She had immense enjoyment in just being part of
their lives and in sharing their company. If both her daughters
were away at the same time she would spend holidays with
some of these friends. Chief amongst these were undoubtedly
Vernon and Morwen Higham of Cardiff. Vernon had exercised
a very fruitful ministry for many years as the minister of Heath
Evangelical Church, Cardiff, one of the largest evangelical
churches in Wales. His closeness to the Doctor was such that it
was he who preached the Doctor's funeral sermon. Ann recalls
that her mother loved spending time with the Highams. Even the
journey from London was something which she enjoyed. It would
begin with Bethan packing her case with meticulous care. She
was a born perfectionist and would place tissue paper between
each layer of clothing to prevent things creasing whilst travelling.
Ann would then drive down the M4 to one of the service stations,
where the Highams would meet them and take Bethan on with

---

16. Quote from Mrs Lloyd-Jones' daughter Ann.

them to their home. This happened twice a year for three weeks at a time.

On one occasion when Mrs Lloyd-Jones was staying at the Highams', it so happened that the wife of a worker at the Heath Church was at their home. As he knew she had been a nurse, Mr Higham shared with this young woman that he was to have an injection that morning. He was a little apprehensive about this and said to the nurse, 'I have to have the injection in my groin,' and then asked, 'Where exactly is my groin?'!

As the former nurse was quite young and this was her *minister*, she felt a bit nonplussed as to how to describe the position of this part of his anatomy. She was relieved, therefore, to see Mrs Lloyd-Jones enter the room, and immediately said to her, 'You were a doctor Mrs Lloyd-Jones. Mr Higham was just asking the location of his groin'.

'Well, yes, your groin is situated on the *inner upper part* of your thigh', Mrs Lloyd-Jones stated with precision.

'Oh', said Mr Higham, patting the upper, outer part of his thigh.

'No, my boy, I said, *INNER!*' was the response from the doctor.

Vernon and Morwen's recollection is that Bethan had simple interests and was very easy to have in the home. They fondly recall that Mrs Lloyd-Jones loved singing Welsh hymns in the bathroom, and each morning they would hear her regale them with the same Welsh hymn as she came down the stairs for breakfast. Her great love was Scrabble, but there was no way that she would play this of an afternoon, even if the weather was very bad: it was definitely an 'after 7' activity! As the evening wore on, however, she could enjoy more mundane things. If a cowboy film happened to be on later in the night, she would stay up with her friends, watching it until midnight, eating bacon sandwiches—what are known in South Wales as 'bacon butties'—and she thoroughly enjoyed the experience!

Something which she particularly liked watching on TV, whether at home or when away, was billiards. She would examine the table and decide the best moves that could possibly be made.

She loved watching it, but found it to be a bit frustrating when she visited a friend in Weston-Super-Mare, because her friend only had a black and white television: colour television for such a programme does make a big difference!

Mrs Lloyd-Jones had many other interests which occupied her in the home. At one time she copied a knitting pattern for a circular skirt: she had laboriously written out every knit and purl stitch by hand! (I can hear you ladies, who know anything about knitting, gasp at this point!) This testifies to a huge amount of patience on her part.

Mrs Lloyd-Jones was a great collector of all manner of things. She had a recipe for home-made blackberry wine. Something else she did for years was to collect stamps, and she also encouraged Elizabeth to do the same. She would place interesting ones in envelopes and eventually sell them, giving the proceeds to missionary organisations. Or she would occasionally send unusual ones to other people. Not long after her husband's operation, in March 1968, Mrs Lloyd-Jones sent a large brown envelope to a woman, who sent the following reply:

> A warm feeling came over me and I said to myself, how kind of you at such a time to take the trouble to send me stamps ... when I opened it my heart sang within me for the Christian love that had prompted you to write to me. Thank you very much for all your care and loving kindness to me.[17]

Bethan's collecting, be it patterns, recipes or stamps, did not stop there: for more than fifty years she kept press cuttings of her husband, which proved to be an invaluable treasure store for Iain Murray in his writing of the Doctor's two-volume biography.

As the above testifies, Mrs Lloyd-Jones had a wealth of interests, but music was not one of them. When it came to classical music, she merely endured it! Her husband once took her to an opera

---

17. Lloyd-Jones Archive: A correspondent to Bethan Lloyd-Jones.

when they were in Rome: although she was captivated by the spectacle, she remembered little about the music and said that she would certainly never go to such a performance again. In this respect her taste was certainly different from that of her husband, who thoroughly enjoyed opera. Indeed, love of opera is something found in the Lloyd-Jones family: Christopher has pointed out that not only did the Doctor's daughters share in his love of opera, but that the Doctor's nephew, David Lloyd-Jones—who became a world authority on Russian music—would become Director of English National Opera North. Although the musical tastes of the Doctor and his wife diverged considerably, it seems that they were able to enjoy listening to some music together. Fascinating information on this—as well as on how the Doctor prepared his sermons—is to be found in the lectures which he gave on preaching at Westminster Theological Seminary in 1969. It seems that earlier in his ministry the Doctor and Mrs Lloyd-Jones used to listen over lunch to a weekly radio programme of new records. The Doctor refers to one occasion when a well-known duet was being sung by two very famous singers, and it seems fairly clear that it was a classical piece which they were singing. Evidently the Doctor was profoundly moved by it.[18] Although he says that he and his wife enjoyed listening to this programme, was this a case where, for his sake, she went along with him? Or was it, rather, that the programme also included popular, as well as classical, music? This far from the event, we shall probably never know the answer to this question; but what we do know is that she rather liked *some* popular music. But there is popular music and then there is *popular* music! Once, when travelling by boat to the U.S., Bethan wrote home, describing her dislike of 'modern' music:

> ... *there is an abominable 'band' which plays incessant execrable 'music', the leader every now and then bursting into so-called song in a voice that has to be heard to be believed—he*

18. Lloyd-Jones (1971), 211–212.

sounds as though he is in mortal agony—moans and bellows
alternatively so that we are <u>very</u> grateful for our cabin.[19]

It would be quite wrong, however, to assume that after the Doctor died, Mrs Lloyd-Jones thought that it was time to 'hang up her boots' and spend all her time doing nothing but playing croquet, watching billiards on television, playing Scrabble, eating 'bacon butties' and watching cowboy films late at night! If she had employed her literary gifts to good effect in translation work while her husband was alive, after his death she began to write her own work. *Memories of Sandfields* was published in 1983.[20] It is a delightful book—written in her own informal, conversational style—in which she lets us into the lives of some of the 'characters' who came to faith in Sandfields during the Doctor's time there. She also gives some fascinating information concerning what church life was like in Aberavon, as well as writing entertainingly about some of the travels which she and the Doctor undertook. It is a perfect blending of the natural and the spiritual. One can only wish that she had been able to have written a similar book about Westminster Chapel. How interesting it would have been! Bethan rose to the challenge of continuing to run the race set before her, without her life's partner: she was to labour on for another ten years.

But godliness with contentment is great gain. For we brought
nothing into the world, and we can take nothing out of it. But
if we have food and clothing, we will be content with that.
1 Timothy 6:6–8

---

19. Lloyd-Jones Archive: Bethan Lloyd-Jones to her family.

20. This book is still in print and can be bought through the Evangelical Movement of Wales bookshops. It is a wonderful read that contains many notable stories of converts at Sandfields, Aberavon.

Bethan Lloyd-Jones, July 1987. (By courtesy of J.Horn.)

Bethan with Revd Vernon Higham, at the graveside of her husband.

12

THROUGH THE PORTALS OF DEATH

Praise be to the God and Father of our Lord Jesus Christ! In
his great mercy he has given us … an inheritance that can
never perish, spoil or fade—kept in heaven for you.
1 PETER 1:3a, 4a

What you leave behind is not what is engraved in stone
monuments, but what is woven into the lives of others.
PERICLES

Family

'What is a family?' is a question which forms the title of a book
by Edith Schaeffer.[1] Martin Luther provided one answer when he
referred to the family, on one particular occasion, as 'the school
for character'. Without doubt, however, a family is many things,
and can be viewed from a number of perspectives. Where God
has blessed a husband and wife with children and then with
grandchildren, the family can be every bit as much 'the place of
comfort' as it can be the school for character, especially when one
of the spouses has been widowed.

---

1. Schaeffer (1976).

Although the Doctor's death had left a vacuum which nobody could fill, Bethan lived a contented, uncomplaining life as a widow, playing a very central part in her family's life. If her children and grandchildren could not take her husband's place, they certainly contributed to her closing years being fulfilled and happy ones. Her love for her own children overflowed to her grandchildren. She spent time listening to all that they wanted to share with her, and they, in turn, were enthralled listening to her: they would sit as she regaled them with tales of places she had visited and things she had done when she was younger. As a consequence of her flat being in the same house as that of her daughter Ann, Ann's three children had the benefit of seeing their grandmother on a daily basis. This, however, did not make the slightest difference to the affection which she had for all six of her grandchildren. Bethan loved them all very much, and was thrilled to have lived long enough to see at least one great-grandchild.

Godliness and a life of service provide no immunity from the effects of age, nor do they necessarily guarantee a glorious exit out of this world. To Enoch and to Elijah alone were granted an entrance into the heavenly realms without having to pass through the portals of death. We know that the Lord took Enoch but are not informed of the mode or manner of his departure. To Elijah was granted a magnificent exit, being taken to heaven in a whirlwind, separated from Elisha by a chariot of fire and fiery horses and the horsemen of Israel. For many of God's people their exit from this world has been much more commonplace: great King David, cold and needing a human 'hot water bottle'; Paul, before his imminent departure, in prison, facing the cold of winter without his cloak, and the absence of those who had deserted him. The end, as far as it is viewed on earth, may appear anything but glorious. How ordinary was the event which 'triggered' the end of the journey for Mrs Lloyd-Jones!

God's grace may enable us to 'handle' our temperament, but it does not essentially change it. Reference has been made in earlier chapters to the tendency to anxiety which Mrs Lloyd-Jones had—and overcame. But neither grace nor the passing of the years removed it entirely. One evening one of her granddaughters had gone out, and Mrs Lloyd-Jones heard her returning later in the evening through the main door by which access was gained both to Ann's flat and to that of Mrs Lloyd-Jones. Although the granddaughter was old enough to be responsible to lock the front door, Bethan was concerned that it had not been locked, so she made her way out of her ground-floor flat—without her Zimmer frame on which to lean—just to check. It *had* been locked. On her way back to her flat she stumbled, fell, and broke her hip. How often does a seemingly insignificant event lead to significant consequences! Mercifully, Ann heard her mother and was able to phone for immediate assistance, and Mrs Lloyd-Jones was rushed into hospital. Surgery was necessary, but although it was successful, there were periods after the operation when she was quite confused. However, a greater part of the time found her laughing and joking with the nurses: godliness can be expressed in very down-to-earth ways in circumstances which are far from congenial. Authentic holiness truly 'humanises' the child of God and brings cheer rather than gloom. Bethan expressed great appreciation of the nursing staff. How often godliness is to be seen in the 'little' things—the thankfulness to people for acts of thoughtfulness and kindness! And godliness has its own beauty: 'the beauty of holiness'. Bethan's beauty was to be seen and acknowledged up to her dying day. Just a few days before she left this world to be with her Saviour, a nurse was overheard commenting upon her beauty. Truly, beauty *is* fleeting; but when God's grace touches a life, it transforms everything. Grace refines nature, and the nurse beheld the beauty of true holiness in Bethan Lloyd-Jones.

But although grateful for the kindness of the nursing staff, Bethan was anxious lest she would have to spend the remainder of her days in a nursing home, and this prompted her to ask her family on a regular basis, 'When am I able to come home?' In the mercy of God this was something which neither she nor her family had to face. Visited regularly by her loved ones, it was Elizabeth who was with her when the call came for her from the One to whom the death of His saints is precious. Many of the family, having contracted a virus that left them feeling very weak almost immediately after the death of Bethan, were quite unwell at the time. In addition to this, London had one of the worst snow storms ever witnessed and, therefore, a large funeral could not be contemplated. And so it was that, in the chapel where, as a young child many years earlier she had witnessed powerful revival scenes, and where ten years earlier hundreds had gathered to pay their last respects to her husband, Vernon Higham led the small, family funeral for Bethan Lloyd-Jones.

Mr Higham had preached the funeral service for the Doctor those ten years earlier on the words which refer to God's people experiencing an 'abundant entrance into the eternal kingdom of our Lord Jesus Christ'.[2] The precise words are all-important: it is not an 'abundant exit' from this world but an 'abundant entrance' or rich welcome into the next to which Peter refers. Bunyan's Christian did not cross the river with the same calmness which characterised Hopeful, but the trumpets on the other side sounded just as much for him as they did for his companion. Mrs Lloyd-Jones' funeral may well have been a much quieter affair than that of her husband, and the commemorative service held for her the following Sunday at Westminster Chapel may not have attracted the thousands who attended for the thanksgiving service for her husband, but from the standpoint of eternity these things are of little consequence. It will not matter there how well we were known on this earth or whether we will be remembered at all when passing from this world. What will matter—and the only thing that will matter—is whether we have known and served the Saviour. And even giving a cup of cold water to one of his people is what he will mark as service.

---

2. 2 Peter 1:11 [KJV]

Shortly after the funeral service at Bethel Chapel, Mrs Lloyd-Jones' earthly remains were taken to the beautiful spot in the Teifi Valley where her husband had been buried and were laid beside him in the same grave in Gelli Cemetery to await, with him, the voice of the archangel and the trumpet call of God on the day of resurrection.

> *But do not forget this one thing, dear friends:*
> *With the Lord a day is like a thousand years,*
> *And a thousand years are like a day ...*
> 2 PETER 3:8

> *For the Lord himself will come down from heaven,*
> *with a loud command, with the voice of the archangel*
> *and with the trumpet call of God,*
> *and the dead in Christ will rise first.*
> *After that, we who are still alive and are left*
> *will be caught up together with them in the clouds*
> *to meet the Lord in the air.*
> *And so we will be with the Lord forever.*
> *Therefore encourage each other with these words.*
> 1 THESSALONIANS 4:16–18

Another four generations: Bethan (right) and her grand-daughter Bethan, daughter Elizabeth and great-grand-daughter Myfanwy.

EPILOGUE:
A TALE OF TWO WOMEN

It is interesting to note the similarities between Susannah Spurgeon and Bethan Lloyd-Jones. Both, as has already been stated, served their Lord and Master by supporting their husbands in their service of Jesus Christ. Both women also helped their respective husbands in their ministry in many practical ways. Mrs Lloyd-Jones would listen patiently as Doctor Lloyd-Jones shared with her relevant parts of discourses or sermons on which he valued her comments. The same help was given by Susannah, who would sit on a Saturday evening surrounded by her husband's books, and read them at will to Spurgeon.

Both women survived their husbands—Susannah by twelve years, Bethan by ten. Both women spent much of their widowhood collecting and sifting notes, sermons etc. to help publish their husbands' life and works.

They both excelled in works of *service to others*. Bethan was always available at the end of a phone for whoever had need of her wise counsel, and she wrote many letters of encouragement to those who were in need. Susannah's pen was never idle as she replied to enquiries concerning the Book Fund which she had begun. (This was started to help poorly paid ministers be able to acquire books which would help them in their ministry; it was a work which later extended help to pastors who were overseas.)

One great difference between these two women was that Bethan Lloyd-Jones was blessed with good health all her life, whereas Susannah Spurgeon was unwell for much of her time on earth.

It is interesting to observe that there were not only similarities between Bethan and Susannah, but also between Martyn Lloyd-Jones and Charles Haddon Spurgeon. Both were men whom God raised up and mightily used in their own generation. Both were great evangelists and leaders of men. Both began their ministries in relatively obscure places, where they saw considerable blessing. Both ministered for many years in London but also travelled extensively to preach God's Word. Both men experienced considerable misunderstanding and misrepresentation from the Lord's own people: Spurgeon in the lacerating 'Down-grade controversy' and Lloyd-Jones in the aftermath of his 1966 address on evangelical unity. In the case of both men, the misunderstanding and misrepresentation continued after their death. And though dead, both men, like Abel of old, still speak to us today. There was, however, at least one great difference between them: Spurgeon, like his wife, was dogged with ill health for many years, whereas the Doctor enjoyed good health for most of his life.

Both Dr Lloyd-Jones and Spurgeon were utterly devoted to their wives, and enjoyed a happy family life. Interestingly both men were, at least on one occasion, absent on the occasion of their wife's birthday. In May 1937 the Doctor was crossing the Atlantic alone. He wrote to his beloved Bethan:

As far as I can remember this is the first time, ever, that I have written to you for your birthday! ... I had endless pleasure in sending it [a telegram], I somehow felt I was in touch with you once more ... I am more certain than ever that there is no one in the world like you, not even approaching you—not in all the world ... I know I am deficient in many things and must at times disappoint you. That really grieves me, and I am trying to improve. But believe me, if you could see my heart you would be amazed at how great is my love.[1]

Similarly Spurgeon wrote to his 'wifey', as he affectionately called her, on one occasion when he was away for her birthday:

I trust this will reach you on your own dear birthday. What an immeasurable blessing you have been to me and are still. Your patience in suffering and diligence in service are works of the Holy Spirit in you for which I adore his Name. Your love to me is not only a product of nature, but it has been so sanctified by grace that it has become a spiritual blessing to me. May you still be upheld, and if you may not be kept from suffering, may you be preserved from sinking.[2]

Great men and great women!

> *Therefore, I urge you … in view of God's mercy, to offer your bodies as living sacrifices, holy and pleasing to God—this is your spiritual act of worship.*
> ROMANS 12:1

---

1. Murray (1990), 781–782.

2. Ray (2006), 237.

QUESTIONS FOR REFLECTION

These are for personal or group use.

CHAPTER 1:
OPEN HOMES AND OPEN HEARTS
FOOD FOR THOUGHT

1. Sometimes we are tempted to think that we can be saved or used by God only if we have a rich spiritual heritage. Nothing could be further from the truth! Obviously there are great benefits in having godly parents or grandparents. Equally there are many examples of God's grace touching and using people whose backgrounds had nothing of true Christian influence. The Lord takes us *as* we are, *where* we are, to use us *as* He will and *when* He will. When and how are we most often in danger of equating spiritual heritage with present godliness?

2. Does the generosity of spirit that we witness in Mr Tom Phillips challenge us? If not, why not?

3. Do spiritual considerations for our children/grandchildren go hand-in-hand with our concern for their material needs?

4. Do we pray that God would revive His work?

> *Brothers [and sisters], pray for us that the message of the Lord may spread rapidly and be honoured, just as it was with you.*
> 2 THESSALONIANS 3:1

5. In this chapter there is evidence of eight-year-old children praying with such fervour in the prayer meeting and listening so attentively to the Word of God. Such attentiveness has to be nurtured in children, and when it is, God may become very real even to very young children. When do we tend to underestimate the work of the Holy Spirit in this manner?

6. Do we have such open homes as those described here? Is our home more like 'a public house without the beer' or 'the house that none-go-by'? How can we make our homes welcoming places to visit and in which to live?

7. The Phillipses obviously maintained a healthy balance between love within the family and concern for those outside the family. Do we maintain both these emphases or are we in danger of stressing one at the expense of the other?

CHAPTER 2:
GIVEN ... A SORT OF GIFT
FOOD FOR THOUGHT

1. Are we so proud of our children that it spills over into 'worldly' boasting and pride?

2. Do we seek to be humble or do we 'enjoy' being conceited and proud?

3. Is our inner beauty more important to us than our outward?

4. Do we covet what others have?

5. Do we use the gifts God has given us or are we slothful and wasteful with such gifts?

CHAPTER 3:
LOVE IS MORE THAN SKIN DEEP
FOOD FOR THOUGHT

1. We are to remember that all our achievements are gifts from God and therefore we have nothing of which to boast. As 1 Corinthians 4:7 asks, 'Who makes you different from anyone else? What do you have that you did not receive?'

What is the biggest motivation for all we do and are? Is it more important to be seen to be 'someone' or are we quite prepared to fade into the background so that God's cause may be advanced?

2. Are we envious of others who, in certain things, are more gifted than we are, or are we glad that God has gifted them in those ways?

3. It is interesting to note that just as some people of a certain stratum of society met in the 1920s around the tennis court, so today in the 2010s it appears that many are meeting through the internet. How is this new venue for meeting both the same as and different from the tennis court?

4. What is my greater *priority* when I view someone of the opposite sex—the outward or the inward?

5. Are most of my arguments with my husband centred on 'Who loves whom the more?' or are they more about being seen to be in the right?

6. Do we think as highly of the 'preaching and pastoral ministry' as did Spurgeon and Dr Lloyd-Jones?

7. What do you think of the statement Dr Lloyd-Jones made: *I had to say Wales came first*?

8. If we believe something to be right and from God, are we willing to stand by it, although everyone else may appear to be against it?

CHAPTER 4:
WIFE FOR ALL SEASONS

FOOD FOR THOUGHT

1. In some cases, a minister is on such a low income that his wife has to work. In other cases a minister may be properly supported, but the cost of living in some areas—one thinks of parts of London, for example—is so high that a wife may need to work simply to help meet basic necessities. Regardless of whether or not we are married to a minister or are currently working outside the home, would we be willing to give up our careers to support our spouse in the work of the gospel, if such a decision were put before us?

2. Are we ever watchful of ways in which we can support and help the ministers of our churches (and the families of our ministers, too!)?

3. Do we regularly give thanks for Christian brothers and sisters like the Robsons, who shared all they had with others?

4. Do we seek to be thoughtful when we are offered hospitality by others? (Just a card of thanks can be an encouragement!)

5. Do we 'live simply so that others may simply live'?

6. Do we ever reflect on incidents that have happened in our lives in which God has safeguarded us from danger or even imminent death? Have we ever recorded such incidents, so that we do not forget God's goodness to us and are further trained to note God's intervention in our lives?

7. Are we thoughtful in the company of those who may have less than us, or do we flaunt our wealth?

8. There are many phobias and fears that the Christian might have, but there is nothing too great or too small that we cannot bring to God. He can deliver us from anything that holds us in its power, because He is the *all*-powerful God. If we have a fearful temperament, do we ask God to help us deal with this area of our lives? How can we seek further dependence upon God in this area?

9. Do we examine our lives, in the light of God's Word, to ensure we are converted and not just religious?

A fascinating book which throws light on Mrs Lloyd-Jones' spiritual condition is *More Than Notion*, written by J.H. Alexander[1]. Interestingly, the Doctor wrote the Foreword to this book and commended it to the congregation at Westminster Chapel as a book which emphasises the importance of true experiential Christianity. *More Than Notion* tells the story of a very 'religious' family who are

---

1. Alexander, 1965.

converted one by one, and bears remarkable similarity to Bethan's experiences before her conversion.

10. 'The Federal Vision' is a term which is used to denote an approach to God's covenant with His people, the Christian life, the church and the place of children within the church which has gathered momentum in certain areas in recent years. This approach emphasises the importance of treating the children of Christian parents as being already Christians and not in need of new birth unless and until they give clear evidence to the contrary[2]. In what ways does the experience of Bethan Lloyd-Jones highlight the grave danger of this approach to Christian experience in general, and to the biblical teaching of conversion in particular?

11. Are we thankful for all God has given us when we consider there are many around us in the world who have so little? Do we daily give thanks to God at the table for our food? If not, why not?

If you only had today what you thanked God for yesterday, what would that be?

12. Ministers, if they are married, should not take offence if their wives constructively and tactfully assess their ministry—better their wives than others! But ministers also need, in equal doses, encouragement.

The minister without a wife needs to search out a good, faithful and loving friend who will be able to point out areas where he can improve, and encourage him when he is down. An accountability friend is worth *his* weight in gold.

If it is, or might become, our responsibility to serve a minister in this way, what would be the most important skills for us to cultivate?

13. Do we love one another sufficiently to be able to criticise one another constructively without taking offence?

---

2. For a balanced and incisive critique of 'The Federal Vision', see Guy Prentiss Waters' *The Federal Vision and Covenant Theology: A Comparative Analysis*.

14. As husbands and wives, are we sufficiently concerned for one another, as was evidently the case with the Lloyd-Joneses?

15. Do we regularly pray for God's servants—for their protection, as well as blessing upon their ministry—as they stand in the front line of battle and face the devil's venomous spite and attacks?

> *For our struggle is not against flesh and blood ... but against the powers of this dark world and against the spiritual forces of evil in the heavenly realms.*
> EPHESIANS 6:12

16. Are we careful to be principled when we are faced with situations that are emotive? How do we face 'controversy'? Do we tackle the problem or the person?

17. Do we put others before ourselves?

18. Do we assure one another—in ways in which we are most comfortable—that we love those who are dear to us?

19. Are we a source of comfort to others?

CHAPTER 5:
'CINDERELLA'S CHARIOT FOR ME'
FOOD FOR THOUGHT

1. What is of paramount importance in our homes?

2. Do we seek to be orderly in our living? This may be second-nature to some—others may have to work harder to achieve it.

3. It is interesting to note how the Doctor balanced his care for his family with his commitment to his preaching engagements. With Bethan's willing sacrifice he sought to honour both. How do we tend to deal with competing demands for our time and attention? Where are some areas we can improve?

4. Those of us who have had to put our own desires for reading, study, etc. on hold when bringing up children or caring for the elderly/disabled can take comfort from the fact that these periods do not last forever. How would it help us to view such responsibilities as new 'marching orders' from the Lord for a specific season?

It should encourage those caring long term for sick children/relatives that each is assigned his/her lot in life—they come in all shapes and sizes, and vary in complexity—but their ultimate purpose is to bring us nearer to God and conform us more to His image. God has shaped our course in life and never intended that we walk alone as His children. Bethan Lloyd-Jones embraced this and that was one of the reasons that she was able to accept all that God brought her way[3].

5. It is so important for parents to be impartial when their children are criticised. All too often, parents can fall into one of two opposite extremes: for some parents, in their eyes, their child is never to blame, while other parents assume their child is always to blame! Truth, for the Christian, is what should matter supremely, not defending our offspring, come what may.

This principle is as equally important when it comes to our spouses. Too easily we can take their part blindly. When dealing with others we should deal with them as we would with our own family.

Can we say that we are impartial in *all* our dealings with others, whether family, friend or foe?

6. Do we tend to be legalistic or antinomian? Do we lay down too many guidelines for our children—or too few? Do we seek to be balanced and principled in guiding our children? What do we base our principles on?

7. Do we place our children and their needs before our own comfort and ease?

8. We are prayerfully to encourage our children, but never to seek to bring them to a premature spiritual birth. How can we discern the difference between these?

---

3. See Appendix 3.

9. If we are married and have children, do we realise what a high calling we have in being a home-maker, whether or not we also work outside the home?

10. Do our concern, love and care follow our children out of the home? How do we show our love for them outside of the home?

11. If our children were asked to name their parents' greatest virtue, what would they say? What if they were asked to name their parents' worst trait?

12. How do we show honour and respect our parents/grand-parents? How do we encourage other families to do the same? How does this differ based on the stage of life or attitudes of our parents/grandparents?

CHAPTER 6:
MINISTRY MATTERS

FOOD FOR THOUGHT

1. With work as demanding as the ministry, a man has to look to his wife for support. Do we agree with this statement? If we are looking to 'carve out our career', will we have the resources to be there to give the support our husbands need?

2. How does the ways that a minister's wife spends her time and energy affect her husband's work of ministry?

3. A minister's work can be undermined if his wife is a gossip. In some cases she can even disqualify him from the ministry. Do you agree?

4. What is involved in a wife's 'giving her husband up' to promote the gospel? Does the husband have any responsibilities to the wife in return?

5. Should a minister's wife have 'special friends' in the church?

6. Is there rivalry in the manse or a genuine support in the work?

The Minister's Wife by Ann Benton and Friends gives food for thought:

> May I suggest that instead of nursing resentment (resentment that the children will quickly pick up on) that you are the one who is always changing the nappies, doing the school run, making the packed lunches, you look on this as a loving contribution which releases your husband into ministry. If he is the major wage-earner he is already making a contribution. I write this not to let fathers off the hook, but to warn women against allowing a root of bitterness to grow up. There may be times when you need to remind your husband of how much you value and need his help and input, but there is also a place for sacrifice, cheerfulness, fortitude and grace. Motherhood is something you do for God.

7. Billy Graham's wife was once asked why she did not join the 'Women's Liberation Movement?' Her reply: 'Billy liberated me years ago!'

8. Do we berate our loved ones, or do we value them for what they can do?

9. Have we ever asked God what He would have us do in/for the church?

10. How can we indicate that we value and prize the opportunity we have to meet regularly with God's people rather than regarding Sunday as 'the Lord's half-day'?

11. Are we able to rise above our circumstances and function with the same grace, whatever our situation?

12. Have we lost the concept of education? Is education wider and broader than merely learning skill?

Some women say, 'If I don't enter the world of paid employment, it's a waste of my education'. If some ministers who have been highly educated were to adopt the same principle, might it not mean that they would never become pastors? Might this mean that the only men who would then become pastors would be those whose only further or higher education consisted of that of training for the gospel ministry? While there is clearly a need and a place for such men, would not the church of Jesus Christ be deprived of His gifts to the church if these were the only men who were to become pastors? What loss the church would have suffered in the twentieth century if Dr Lloyd-Jones had remained a physician! What loss the church of the twentieth century and of today would have suffered if Don Carson had remained a chemist! How might the experiences of these men illuminate the experiences of educated women?

13. Is there a difference between helping the family economy and wanting to provide 'luxuries' for them? How does this play out in practice?

14. Are we as solicitous over one another as the Bible commands us to be? Look at Philippians 2:3b-5.

15. Have we ever considered that some Christians in countries where there is no religious freedom to worship God take their very lives in their hands when they seek to meet with God's people week by week?

16. Are we given to hospitality? Consider the teaching found in the following verses: Matthew 25:35–36; Acts 16:15; Romans 12:13, 16:23; 1 Timothy 3:2, 5:10; 1 Peter 4:9; 3 John 8.

17. Do we pray daily for all the resources the Lord has promised us, in order to live a life that will bring glory to Him?

CHAPTER 7:
OVER TWENTY YEARS OF LIFE
FOOD FOR THOUGHT

1. Are we concerned for our ageing parents?

The following two statements concerning 'the old' may provoke further reflection. The first is by a journalist, Tom Utley, who commented in a feature for *The Daily Telegraph* that Britain's old people would be much better off in Africa. He says:

There is, as we all know, a very much better way of looking after the elderly than simply shovelling money in the direction of strangers, in the hope that they will look after them. I am thinking of the most effective social security system ever devised by man or nature. It is a system that still operates in most primitive societies, but one which is on the verge of collapse in modern Britain. I mean, of course, the family. In almost every way, I would much rather live here than in a mud-hut in Africa. But I reckon that the very old in the Third World, looked after by their families in communities bustling with life, have a much better time of it than a great many British OAPs [Old Age Pensioners], sitting around in care homes stinking of urine, watching afternoon television and counting the days or weeks until that rare visit from their young.[4]

The second article is in a challenging essay on this subject by the American writer Walter Wangerin. He writes:

The commandments have not expired. Nor have the holy promises that attend them been abolished. When, therefore, I am asked regarding the future of some human community, some family, some nation—or the Church, the visible Church itself!—straight-way I look for obedience to the commands of God. Particularly I wonder regarding the one which urges honour for the parents: I look to see whether someone is singing songs to his aged mother—and if I can find him, I say, 'The signs are good'. This is no joke. The best prognostication for the life of any community—whether it shall be long or short—is not financial, political, demographic … It is moral. Ask not, 'How strong is the nation?' nor 'How many are they? How well organised? With what armies and resources?' Ask rather, 'How does this people

---

4. Benton, 2007, 13.

behave ... Do we as a people honour our mothers and fathers? Do we honour the generation that has raised us—especially when it sinks down into an old and seemingly dishonourable age? ... 'The question is not irrelevant to our future, whether we shall have one or not. That it may be well with you and you may live long on the earth.[5]

2. What we expect from life has shifted somewhat over the years. The expectation of many of our forefathers was to live a godly life. What is our expectation?

> *Religion that God our Father accepts as pure and faultless is this: to look after orphans and widows in their distress and to keep oneself from being polluted by the world.*
> JAMES 1:27

3. It is good to consider the needs of our families when they are old and infirm, and if it lies within our power and capabilities, to put their needs before our own. Discuss.

CHAPTER 8:
WONDERFUL WAY WITH WORDS
FOOD FOR THOUGHT

1. Have we concern that *all types* of people come to know the Lord Jesus Christ? How is that concern reflected in our actions and decisions?

2. Do we show love and practical help for the 'odd-ones' who may be in our churches or do we simply avoid them? Why?

3. Do we use the gifts God has given us—whatever they may be?

4. Are we considerate towards others and do we pray for them, even when they are out of sight?

5. Does our concern for others radiate further than from our own homes?

---

5. ibid., 18–19.

6. Virtues we need to pray for daily as Christians are: *love*—the Bible never wearies of telling us this;—and *wisdom*—we'll not be 'scolded' for asking for it. We are also commanded to *seek* wisdom, as it 'is more precious than rubies'(Proverbs 8:11). Discernment is requisite too.

> *You do not have because you do not ask God.*
> JAMES 4:2b

7. Do we realise how much time we can waste, watching what God is doing in other people's lives, rather than getting on with what God wants us to do for Him?

> *Peter turned and saw that the disciple whom Jesus loved was following them … When Peter saw him, he asked, 'Lord, what about him?' '… what is that to you? You must follow Me.'*
> JOHN 21:20–22.

8. Do we think about and think through the things we do, in relation to the Bible's teaching?

> *…whatever is true, whatever is noble, whatever is right, whatever is pure, whatever is lovely, whatever is admirable—if anything is excellent or praiseworthy— think about such things.*
> PHILIPPIANS 4:8

9. Are we gifted in letter writing? How do we communicate encouragement to others when we are not with them in person?

Have we considered writing letters to imprisoned believers in the Third World and/or letter writing to prisoners in this country or abroad? How else could we use the power of written words to reach out to others?

CHAPTER 9:
IN JOURNEYINGS OFTEN
FOOD FOR THOUGHT

1. Are we concerned for the spiritual well-being of our nation—wherever that may be in God's world?

2. Are we willing to be sacrificial so that others may share what we have?

3. Are we content with what God has given to us or are we always hankering after more?

4. If we are not married, obviously we shall not be called to 'give up' our husbands. But are we not called upon to give up our time, our money, our gifts, so that others may benefit? How does such sacrifice take place both within and outside of marriage?

5. Do we 'trust in the Lord' when we are afraid, cast down, weary, lacking confidence, etc.?

6. Do we come with an eager anticipation and expectation to hear God's Word?

7. Do we rightly appreciate our spiritual leaders?

> *... who work hard among you, who are over you in the Lord ... Hold them in the highest regard in love because of their work.*
> 1 THESSALONIANS 5:12–13

8. Are we generous in our giving or do we give grudgingly?

> *God loves a cheerful giver.*
> 2 CORINTHIANS 9:7

9. Is our warmth of love towards others noticed, even in old age?

10. Have we good friends? If not, why not? If we have, do we invest in them?

11. Do we work hard for the Lord, if we have the health, even into old age? If we do, do we remember to 'come aside and rest awhile', so that we can continue in our labours?

12. Do we delight in God's creation?

Heaven above is softer blue, earth around is sweeter green;
Something lives in every hue Christless eyes have never seen ...[6]

13. Is our spiritual life natural, and is our natural life spiritual?

CHAPTER 10:
EVER-WIDENING CIRCLES
FOOD FOR THOUGHT

1. Is our Christian practice based on the Word of God or tradition?

2. It is important that we do not sin against our conscience, or be *the cause* of someone sinning in this way.

3. Do we, as Christians, think it paramount to familiarise ourselves with *the whole* of the Bible?

4. Do we read the Bible *every* day? If not, why not?

5. Do our prayers consist of our immediate family and friends, or do they extend 'to the butcher' and further afield?

6. If we are married, do we make it a daily practice to read the Bible with our spouse? If not, why not?

7. What do you think of Dr John Kennedy's understanding of Psalm 25:14: *The secret of the Lord is with them that fear him* (AV)? [7]

8. Do we give regularly to the Lord a portion of all that He has given us? Do we do so thoughtfully, consistently? Do we give to others who are in need? How do we understand our Lord's words: *Freely you have received; freely give* (Matt. 10:8b)?

---

6. George Wade Robinson, 'Loved with everlasting love'. *Christian Hymns* 654.

7. Kennedy (1979), 201.

9. Are we careful with *all* that the Lord has entrusted to us?

10. Do we seek counsel from others about decisions we have to make?

11. Do we pray to be wise, not just for our own sake, but for the sake of others who may look to us for counsel?

> *But the wisdom that comes from heaven is first of all pure;*
> *then peace-loving, considerate, submissive, full of mercy and*
> *good fruit, impartial and sincere.*
> JAMES 3:17

CHAPTER 11:
TIME TO PUT ONE'S FEET UP?

FOOD FOR THOUGHT

1. If we are older (or if we are younger!) and have a good measure of health, do we ask God to show us what He would have us to do further for Him? How can we discern this?

2. Are we seeking to encourage those around us who may be passing through trials and tribulations?

3. If we have retired, do we—in the words of Dr Douglas Johnson—'spend a great deal of the week reading'? Why or why not?

4. Do we use the gifts/talents God has given us or do we hide them?

5. Are we willing to open our homes and hearts to those who may be in need—to those well known or to those who are seemingly insignificant?

6. Do we ask God to make us thoughtful and considerate in all we do?

7. Does our love for others, even when we have to sacrifice our 'own time', motivate us in the things we do for them?

8. Do we take note of God's kindly care for us as His children?

Corrie ten Boom, in the following extract from her book,[8] does just that:

> When I was in the German concentration camp at Ravens-
> bruck, one bitter winter morning I woke up with a bad cold.
> Back in Holland I would have been able to adjust to a cold,
> because I would have a tissue or a hankie to blow my nose.
> But in the concentration camp, and without a hankie, I felt
> I could not stand it.
>
> 'Well, why don't you pray for a hankie?' my sister Betsie
> asked.
>
> I started to laugh. There we were, with the world falling
> apart around us. We were locked in a camp where thousands
> of people were being executed each week, being beaten to
> death, or put through unbearable suffering—and Betsie
> suggested I pray for a hankie! If I were to pray for anything,
> it would be for something big, not something little, like that.
>
> But before I could object, Betsie began to pray,
>
> 'Father, in the name of Jesus, I now pray for a hankie for
> Corrie, because she has a bad cold.'
>
> I shook my head and walked away. Very shortly after, I was
> standing by the window when I heard someone call my name.
> I looked out and spotted a friend of mine, another prisoner,
> who worked in the hospital.
>
> 'Here you are,' she said in a matter-of-fact tone. 'Take it,
> I bring you a little present.'
>
> I opened the little parcel, and inside was a handkerchief!
> I could hardly believe my eyes.
>
> 'How did you know? Did Betsie tell you? Did you know
> I had a cold?'
>
> She shrugged. 'I know nothing. I was busy sewing
> handkerchiefs out of an old sheet, and there was a voice in

---

8. Corrie ten Boom (1985), 197.

my heart saying, "Take a hankie to Corrie ten Boom." So, there is your gift from God.'

That pocket handkerchief, made from an old piece of sheet, was a message from heaven for me. It told me that there is a heavenly Father who hears, even if one of His children on this little planet prays for a tiny little thing like a hankie. Not only does He hear, but He speaks to another of His children and says, 'Bring a hankie to Corrie ten Boom.'

9. It has been said by someone who was widowed that one of the hardest things to come to terms with is the fact that one is no longer the 'number one' person in another's affections—even if one has children or close friends. Discuss.

10. It is not weakness to show our humanity—even the Son of God wept. Discuss.

11. Do we bear with the aged when their propensity to worry grows with age?

Read Ecclesiastes 12:1–8 again, especially 12:3, 5a which follows:

… when the keepers of the house tremble, and the strong men [women] stoop, when the grinders cease because they are few, and those looking through the windows grow dim … when men [women] are afraid of heights and of dangers in the streets …

CHAPTER 12:
THROUGH THE PORTALS OF DEATH
FOOD FOR THOUGHT

1. Are our lives characterised by gratitude?

2. Will we have an 'abundant entrance'?

3. We need to imitate *only* those who imitate Jesus Christ. Who fits this description in our immediate or broader circles?

4. Do we love and follow the Lord Jesus Christ? Do we obey His Word and do what He commands? What are the most common obstacles to this?

5. If Christ has saved us, what 'manner' of life ought we to live? Discuss.

At one time we too were foolish, disobedient, deceived and enslaved by all kinds of passions and pleasures. We lived in malice and envy, being hated and hating one another. But when the kindness and love of God our Saviour appeared, he saved us, not because of righteous things we had done, but because of his mercy. He saved us through the washing of rebirth and renewal by the Holy Spirit, whom he poured out on us generously through Jesus Christ our Saviour, so that, having been justified by his grace, we might become heirs having the hope of eternal life.
This is a trustworthy saying. And I want you to stress these things, so that those who have trusted in God may be careful to devote themselves to doing what is good. These things are excellent and profitable for everyone.
Titus 3:3–8

APPENDICES

APPENDIX 1

CHAPTER 1:
OPEN HOMES AND OPEN HEARTS

Christmas Evans in relation to Evan Phillips

The Welsh Biography Online at The National Library of Wales states that Evan Phillips was a second cousin of Christmas Evans. Tim Shenton, however, in his thoroughly researched biography of Christmas Evans, notes that Christmas's father Samuel had a brother named Daniel. Daniel was the father of the Methodist preacher Daniel Evans, 'who in turn became the grandfather of Evan Phillips'[1]. This, of course, means that Christmas Evans was a first cousin to Evan Phillips' grandfather, and it follows, therefore, that Evan Phillips was a first cousin twice removed of Christmas Evans. The fact that the more famous preacher was born in 1766, whereas Evan Phillips was not born until 1829—a period of 56 years separating their births—should make it fairly obvious that it would be unlikely for them to be second cousins, the definition of second cousins being that they are the respective children of those who are first cousins.

---

1. Shenton (2001), 46.

APPENDIX 2

CHAPTER 4:
WIFE FOR ALL SEASONS

'Another godly woman'

The following example of a 'godly woman' was, in part, the result of Dr Lloyd-Jones encouraging the congregation at Bethlehem, Sandfields, to have a concern for foreign missions. Mrs Violet Robson was the neighbour/friend/church member who was a 'mother in Israel' to Mrs Lloyd-Jones when she lived in Port Talbot. The Doctor did not reckon that some would do *so much* for the needs of brothers and sisters in other lands.

'Mrs Violet Robson, convicted of the amount of money she had long spent on her dress and appearance, sold all her jewellery apart from her wedding ring! A piece of paper, found by her family after her death, revealed that she did not do this without first giving her own self to the Lord, as Christians before her in Corinth [sic] (1 [sic] Corinthians 8:5). In part, her solemn covenant read:

Having had this morning, April 12, 1932, a fresh revelation of my hopeless inability to keep the Law, and that Jesus Christ the Son of the most High God was the fulfilment of the Law, and gave himself to save me from its terror, I desire with all my mind, heart and strength to consecrate myself and everything I hold dear and that I possess . . . I consecrate myself, mind, soul, strength, to the will and purpose of my Heavenly Father and his Son Jesus Christ, by being humble, consistent, faithful, long-suffering, truthful, careful in small things, patient, tolerant and no 'respecter of persons'. Honest in the sight of all men, prayerful, to make myself of no reputation, that Jesus Christ might be glorified and that I may be accounted worthy of the fellowship of his sufferings. Amen.'

APPENDIX 3

CHAPTER 5:
'CINDERELLA'S CHARIOT FOR ME'

Poem: 'Lean Hard' by May Prentiss Smith (1857–1925)

> Child of my love, lean hard,
> And let me feel the pressure of your care;
> I know your burden, child.
> I shaped it;
> Poised it in my own hand;
> Made no proportion in its weight
> To your unaided strength,
> For even as I laid it on, I said,
> 'I shall be near, and while she leans on me,
> This burden shall be mine, not hers;
> So shall I keep my child
> Within the circling arms of my own love.'
> Here, lay it down, nor fear
> To impose it on a shoulder which upholds
> The government of worlds.
> Yet closer come; you are not near enough.
> I would embrace your care;
> So I might feel my child reposing on my breast.
> You love me? I knew it. Doubt not then;
> But loving me, lean hard.

APPENDIX 4

CHAPTER 6:
MINISTRY MATTERS

Elizabeth, even as a young child, had a sense that God was wonderfully at work in Aberavon: 'When I look back on it,' she recalls now, 'my awareness is of the presence of God . . . a sense of glory.' There was a 'radiant sense' in which even a child 'knew that God was there'

The Bethlehem, Sandfields was one of these churches, Aberavon being one of the sea-board towns in South Wales, with busy docks.

One of the men who was to join John Pugh in the work was Seth Joshua. Through his family, his influence reached far afield, into the twentieth century, as the following quotation indicates:

'Peter [Seth Joshua's son] was to spend a long life time in the States that extended into his nineties. His distinguished ministry included preaching at the college graduation of the young Billy Graham. The doyen of post second world war American evangelical scolars, Dr Carl F. Henry, acknowledges the way God used Peter in his own life.

"I heard him preach numerous times before and after I became a believer, in the days when modernism was regnant [sic], and he faithfully proclaimed the gospel. After I became a believer (I was a newspaper reporter and editor) he frequently prodded me toward the ministry. He would say he covered Long Island for the Lord, whereas I covered it for the press. He was a fervent expository preacher of the gospel.

APPENDIX 5

CHAPTER 10:
EVER-WIDENING CIRCLES

Robert Murray M'Cheyne's Reading Scheme

The 19th Century Scottish minister, Robert Murray M'Cheyne, who lived from 1813-1843, prepared a plan for Bible reading to take readers through the New Testament and Psalms twice a year, and through the rest of the Bible once each year.

A copy of this plan can be found via the following website:-

http://www.esv.org/assets/pdfs/rp.one.year.tract.pdf

APPENDIX 6

CHAPTER 10:
EVER-WIDENING CIRCLES

Lachlan Mackenzie (1754–1819) was a powerful preacher who was greatly used of God. He was regarded by the people he served as being possessed of prophetic powers. Certainly, his famous sermon, 'The Babe in Bethlehem', while not being the most rigorous message from an exegetical standpoint, was remarkable for the detailed predictions it gave concerning numerous families in the parish.[2] On the other hand, Kenneth Macrae (1883–1964) had cause to lament one baleful consequence of Mackenzie's 'flock' regarding him as a prophet. In 1924 Macrae—who pastored churches in Scotland from 1915 until his death in 1964, including the large Free Church of Scotland congregation in Stornoway, Lewis, from 1931 to 1964—confided in his diary his dismay at the lack of expectation of blessing in that generation on the part of the people in the Kilmuir congregation. The reason for this, he wrote, was as follows: 'Most of the Kilmuir men put all hope of blessing to a far future date because a godly man has said that the dawn of the latter-day glory would break upon the sword of the butcher, red with the blood of the saints'[3]. Iain Murray, the editor of Macrae's published diary, notes the following in a footnote: 'The reference is to a renewal of persecution inspired by the Papacy. The opinion here expressed was the view of Lachlan MacKenzie (1754–1819), who was commonly credited in the Highlands with prophetic powers[4].

---

2. This, and other unusual features of Mackenzie's ministry, are detailed on pages 60–66 in Kennedy (1979), 60–66.

3. Murray (1980).

4. cf. The Rev. Mr Lachlan of Lochcarron, James Campbell, (1928), pp. 416–417. (ibid., note 1, p. 195, note 1)

APPENDIX 7

CHAPTER 10:
EVER-WIDENING CIRCLES

The murder was committed between six and seven in the morning. Alexander Peden was then ten or eleven miles distant. Before eight o'clock he found himself at the gate of a friend's house, and lifted the latch, and entered the kitchen, craving permission to pray with the family. 'Lord,' he said, 'when wilt Thou avenge Brown's blood? O, let Brown's blood be precious in Thy sight!' When the voice of yearning and entreaty had ceased, John Muirhead, the father in the home, asked Peden what he meant by Brown's blood. 'What do I mean?' he answered. 'Claverhouse has been at the Priesthill this morning, and has murdered John Brown. His corpse is lying at the end of his house, and his poor wife sitting weeping by his corpse, and not a soul to speak comfortably to her.' And then, lifted into a kind of ecstasy, he continued, 'This morning, after the sun-rising, I saw a strange apparition in the firmament, the appearance of a very bright, clear, shining star fall from heaven to the earth. And indeed there is a clear, shining light fallen this day, the greatest Christian that ever I conversed with...' Into Peden's eyes 'from the well of life three drops' were instilled; his heart, as the Quaker apostle said, was baptized into a sense of all conditions; and he saw, by a spiritual intuition, the sorrows which were happening in other parts of the vineyard of Christ[5].

---

5. From Smellie (1960), 407–8.

APPENDIX 8

CHAPTER 11:
TIME TO PUT ONE'S FEET UP?

The hymn Mrs Lloyd-Jones was asked to translate—which the Doctor translated—in English and in Welsh

1. Oh! for that peace, beyond all understanding
   Peace heavenly peace, bought by eternal pain,
   That my frail soul, beneath life's cruel pounding
   At rest at Jesus' Cross may still remain.

2. Oh! give the peace, that in the stormiest fight
   Can never tire and still is amply blest
   So that my soul in midst of blackest night
   Can rest on God, my heavenly Father's breast.

3. Grant me the peace that leads to sweet endeavour
   In heavenly work, in disappointment's hour
   Without a fear, but resting in the favour
   Of God's love and spite of stormy weather.

4. Oh! for the peace, that like that river flowing,
   Through Heavenly City and the Trees of Life
   Peace after war, to Heavenward pilgrim's going
   Beyond the vale, to joy and end of strife.

1. Rho im yr hedd, na wyr y byd amdano,
   Y nefol hedd a ddaeth trwy ddwyfol loes;
   Pan fyddo'r don ar f'enaid gwan yn curo,
   Mae'n dawel gyda'r Iesu wrth y groes.

2. O! dyro'r hedd, na all y stormydd garwaf
   Ei flino byth, na chwerwi ei fwynhad;
   Pan fyddo'r enaid, ar y noson dduaf,
   Yn gwneud ei nyth ym mynwes Duw ein Tad.

3. Rho brofi'r hedd a wna in weithio'n dawel
   Yng ngwaith y nef, dan siomedigaeth flin:
   Heb ofni dim, ond beunydd yn ddiogel
   Yn ymyl Duw, er garwed fyddo'r hin.

4. O! am yr hedd sy'n llifo megis afon,
   Trwy ddinas Duw, dan gangau'r bywiol bren:
   Yr hedd sy'n llenwi bywyd yr angylion:
   Yr hedd fydd inni'n nefoedd byth. Amen.

The hymn-writer was 'Elfed': his full name was H. Elfet Lewis (1860–1953). His hymns are regarded as orthodox and 'sweet', with some truly memorable lines, but tending towards the sentimental and lacking the doctrinal depth and devotional warmth of earlier generations of hymn-writers. He wrote a book on the 1904–05 revival entitled *With Christ among the Miners*.

APPENDIX 9

CHAPTER 11:
TIME TO PUT ONE'S FEET UP?

To what extent was Bethan Lloyd-Jones Edwardian?

It is worth noting that Mrs Lloyd-Jones was less formal than the Doctor. The fact that she referred to him as 'Martyn', rather than 'Doctor' or 'my husband', is indicative of this. This feature of their relationship came home to me back in the 1980s, when my husband and I were staying at John and Mari Jones' farmhouse in Llanymawddwy. There were a number of volumes by the Doctor on one of the bookshelves. These had obviously been gifts from him or Mrs Lloyd-Jones. While the Doctor was alive, he had written something in Welsh in the inside cover and then signed it 'D.M. Lloyd-Jones'. After he died, Bethan had written in Welsh in the inside cover of books which had been published after her husband's death, but, significantly, had signed herself 'Bethan' or 'Bethan Lloyd-Jones'. [I cannot now recall whether it was only her Christian name or her Christian name and surname which she used.] The significant thing is that the Doctor hardly ever signed himself as 'Martyn' when addressing those outside the family circle. In his published letters there are only two letters to someone outside the family where he signed his name as simply 'Martyn'. They were both to his long time medical friend, Gerald Golden. Evidently, then, in some areas, Bethan was less formal than he.

APPENDIX 10

AUTHOR'S QUOTATIONS AT THE BEGINNING
OF EACH CHAPTER:

PROLOGUE:
A SMILE IN PLACE OF TEARS
C.T. studd

Charles Thomas Studd, often known as C.T. Studd (1860–1931), came from a very wealthy family. Educated at Cambridge, he played cricket for England in the 1882 match which was won by Australia and which was the origin of the Ashes. He renounced his fortune and went as a missionary to China, being one of the Cambridge Seven. He also served the Lord in India, and later was responsible for setting up the Heart of Africa Mission, which became the Worldwide Evangelisation Crusade, now W.E.C. International. He famously said: *Some want to live within the sound of church or chapel bell; I want to run a rescue shop within a yard of hell.*

CHAPTER 1:
OPEN HOMES AND OPEN HEARTS
C.S. Lewis

Clive Staples Lewis (1898–1963), commonly known as C.S. Lewis, and known to his friends and family as 'Jack', was a novelist, poet, academic, medievalist, literary critic, essayist, lay theologian and Christian apologist. He is best known for his fictional work, especially *The Screwtape Letters, The Chronicles of Narnia* and *The Space Trilogy,* and for his non-fiction Christian apologetics, such as *Mere Christianity, Miracles* and *The Problem of Pain.*

CHAPTER 2:
GIVEN ... A SORT OF GIFT
Minna Antrim

Minna Thomas Antrim (1861–1950) was an American writer. She is famous for the quote: *Experience is a great teacher, but she sends in terrific bills.* She was well known for her collection of 'toasts' (1902) as well as for her books for children such as *Don'ts for Girls* and *Don'ts for Boys.*

CHAPTER 3:
LOVE IS MORE THAN SKIN DEEP
Helen Keller

Helen Adams Keller (1880–1968) was an American author, political activist and lecturer. She was the first deaf-blind person to earn a Bachelor of Arts degree. A prolific author, Keller was well travelled and outspoken in her convictions. Her birthday on June 27 is commemorated as Helen Keller day in the state of Pennsylvania in the U.S.; this celebration was authorised by President Jimmy Carter in 1980, on the 100th anniversary of her birth.

CHAPTER 4:
A WIFE FOR ALL SEASONS
J.I. Packer

James Innell Packer (1926–) is a well-known evangelical theologian. He became Professor of Systematic and Historical Theology at Regent College in 1979. In 1989, he was installed as the first Sangwoo Youtong Chee Professor of Theology. In 1996, he became Board of Governors' Professor of Theology. J.I. Packer has preached and lectured widely in Great Britain and North America, and is a frequent contributor to theological periodicals. His writings include: *Fundamentalism and the Word of God, Evangelism and the Sovereignty of God, Knowing God, Growing in Christ, God Has Spoken, Knowing Man, Beyond the Battle for the Bible, God's Words, Keep in Step with the Spirit, Christianity the True Humanism, Your Father Loves You, Hot Tub Religion, A Quest for Godliness, Rediscovering Holiness, Concise Theology, A Passion For Faithfulness* and *Knowing Christianity.* He is a member of the Editorial Council of *Christianity Today.* He was General Editor of the English Standard Version of the Bible, first published in 2001.

CHAPTER 5:
'CINDERELLA'S CHARIOT FOR ME'
Samuel Rutherford

Samuel Rutherford (c. 1600–1661) was a Scottish Presbyterian pastor, theologian and author. He was chosen as one of the four main Scottish Commissioners to the Westminster Assembly of Divines in London, taking part in formulating the Westminster Confession of Faith in 1647. His epitaph on his tombstone concluded: *Acquainted with Immanuel's song.*

CHAPTER 6:
MINISTRY MATTERS
Martin Luther King

Martin Luther King, Jr (1929–1968) was an American pastor, activist, humanitarian and leader in the African-American Civil Rights Movement. He is best known for his role in the advancement of civil rights using non-violent civil disobedience based on his Christian beliefs. He was born Michael King, but his father changed his name in honour of the German reformer Martin Luther. King also helped to organise the 1963 March on Washington, where he delivered his famous 'I have a Dream' speech. There he established his reputation as one of the greatest orators in American history.

CHAPTER 7:
OVER TWENTY YEARS OF LIFE
Mark Twain

Samuel Langhorne Clemens (1835–1910), better known by his pen name Mark Twain, was an American author and humourist. He wrote *The Adventures of Tom Sawyer* (1876) and its sequel, *Adventures of Huckleberry Finn* (1885), the latter often called 'the Great American Novel'. In the wake of financial setbacks, he filed for protection from his creditors via bankruptcy, and with the help of a friend overcame his financial troubles. Twain chose to pay all his pre-bankruptcy creditors in full, although he had no legal responsibility to do so.

CHAPTER 8:
WONDERFUL WAY WITH WORDS
Murray M'Cheyne

Robert Murray M'Cheyne (pronounced *Mak-Shayn*, occasionally spelled McCheyne, 1813–1843) was a godly minister in the Church of Scotland from 1835 to 1843. His early death at the age of twenty-nine was caused by typhus, which he contracted during an epidemic spread of this disease. Not long after his death, his friend Andrew Alexander Bonar wrote his biography, which was published with some of his manuscripts and letters as *The Memoirs and Remains of Robert Murray M'Cheyne*. The book sold widely. It has had a lasting influence on evangelical Christianity worldwide. M'Cheyne designed a widely used system for reading through the Bible in one year. The plan entails reading the New Testament and Psalms through twice a year and the Old Testament through once.

CHAPTER 9:
THE DETAIL OF LITTLE THINGS
Corrie ten Boom

Cornelia 'Corrie' ten Boom (1892–1983) was a Dutch Christian who, along with her father and other family members, protected many Jews during the Nazi occupation of Holland. When this was discovered she, together with other members of her family, was sent to a concentration camp. Her famous book, *The Hiding Place*, describes the ordeal. Casper ten Boom (her father) worked as a watchmaker and in 1924 Corrie became the first licensed female watchmaker in the Netherlands. She also helped teach people with learning difficulties, raised foster children in her home and did other charitable works. She was a woman with great faith, great love for her Lord and for people, and a woman with a great heart.

CHAPTER 10:
EVER WIDENING CIRCLES
John Bunyan

John Bunyan (1628–1688) was an English Puritan preacher and writer. He is the author of the immortal work *The Pilgrim's Progress*, arguably the most famous published Christian allegory. In addition to *The Pilgrim's Progress*' Bunyan wrote nearly sixty titles, many of them expanded sermons. He preferred to face and endure twelve years of imprisonment at great sacrifice to himself and his family, rather than resign himself to giving up preaching.

CHAPTER 11:
A TIME TO PUT ONE'S FEET UP?
Elizabeth Elliott

Elizabeth Elliott (1926–) is a Christian author and speaker. Her first husband, Jim Elliott, was killed in 1956 while attempting to make missionary contact with the Auca (now known as Huaorani) of Eastern Equador. She later spent two years as a missionary to the tribe member who killed her husband. Returning to the U.S. after many years in South America, she became widely known as the author of over twenty books and as a speaker in constant demand. Elliott toured the country, sharing her knowledge and experience well into her seventies.

CHAPTER 12:
THROUGH THE PORTALS OF DEATH
Pericles

Pericles (c. 495–429 B.C.) was a leader in ancient Athens. He was a great orator, his most famous speech being given at the funeral of the first citizens to die in the Peloponnesian War.

BIBLIOGRAPHY

Alexander, 1965: Alexander, J.H. *More Than Notion*. Zoar Publications, Second Edition (Ossett, 1965).

Catherwood, 1988: Catherwood, C. *Martyn Lloyd-Jones: Chosen by God*. Highland Books (Crowborough, East Sussex, 1988).

Catherwood, 1995: Catherwood, C. *A Family Portrait*. Kingsway Publications Ltd. (Eastbourne, East Sussex, 1995).

Catherwood, 1996: Catherwood, Sir F. *At the Cutting Edge*. Hodder & Stoughton (London, 1996)

Clark, 2004: Clark, S. 'The 1904 Revival—or was it? (In '*The Faith that Saves*', The Westminster Conference 2004) (Great Britain, 2004).

Davies, 1984: Davies, J.E. *Striving Together: The Evangelical Movement of Wales—Its Principles and Aims*. Evangelical Press of Wales (Bridgend, Mid-Glamorgan, 1984).

Evans, 1987: Evans, E. *The Welsh Revival of 1904*. Bryntirion Press. (Bridgend, Mid-Glamorgan, 1987).

Fielder, 1983: Fielder, G.D. *'Excuse me, Mr. Davies- Hallelujah!':* *Evangelical Student Witness in Wales 1923–1983*. Evangelical Press of Wales. InterVarsity Press (Bridgend, Mid-Glamorgan and Leicester, 1983).

Fielder, 2000: Fielder, G. *Grace, Grit & Gumption*. Christian Focus Publications and The Evangelical Movement of Wales (Ross-shire, Scotland and Bridgend, Wales, 2000).

Gibbard, 2002: Gibbard, N. *The History of the Evangelical Movement of Wales 1948–98*. Bryntirion Press (Bridgend, Mid-Glamorgan, 2002).

Jones, 1984: Jones, G.F. Cows, *Cardies and Cockneys.* Self-published by Camelot (Borth, Dyfed. SY24 5LD).

Jones, 1976: Jones, M. *In the Shadow of Aran*. Evangelical Movement of Wales (Bridgend, Mid-Glamorgan, 1972).

Jones, 1979: Jones, J. & M. *In the Shelter of the Fold*. Bryntirion Press (Bridgend, Mid-Glamorgan 1979).

Jones, 1992: Jones, J. & M. *When Swallows Return*. Bryntirion Press (Bridgend, Mid-Glamorgan 1992).

Kennedy, 1979: Kennedy, J. *The Days of the Fathers of Ross-shire.* Christian Focus Publications (Inverness, 1979).

Lloyd-Jones, 1983: Lloyd-Jones B. *Memories of Sandfields*. The Banner of Truth Trust (Edinburgh, 1983).

Lloyd-Jones, Sept. 1987: Lloyd-Jones, B. My Memories of the 1904-05 Revival in Wales. Part 1. Evangelicals Now—Sept. (Great Britain, 1987).

Lloyd-Jones, Oct. 1987: Lloyd-Jones, B. My Memories of the 1904-05 Revival in Wales. Part 11. Evangelicals Now—Oct. (Great Britain, 1987).

Lloyd-Jones, 1970: Lloyd-Jones, D.M. *Romans. Exposition of Chapter 3:20–4:25, Atonement and Justification.* The Banner of Truth Trust (Edinburgh, 1970).

Lloyd-Jones, 1971: Lloyd-Jones, D.M. *Preaching & Preachers.* Hodder and Stoughton (London, 1971).

Lloyd-Jones, 1976: Lloyd-Jones, D.M. Jonathan Edwards and the Crucial Importance of Revival.

Lloyd-Jones, D.M. *Romans. Exposition of Chapter 14:1–17. Liberty and Conscience.* The Banner of Truth Trust (Edinburgh, 2003).

Morgan, 1973: Morgan, *E. John Elias: Life and Letters.* The Banner of Truth Trust (Edinburgh, 1973).

Morgan, J.J. Cofiant *E. Phillips/The Life of E. Phillips.* Published by the family (Sunnyside, 1930).

Murray, 1980: Murray, I.H. *Diary of Kenneth Macrae.* The Banner of Truth Trust (Edinburgh, 1980).

Murray, 1982: Murray, I.H. D. Martyn Lloyd-Jones. *The First Forty Years,1899–1939.* The Banner of Truth Trust (Edinburgh, 1982).

Murray, 1990: Murray I.H. D. Martyn Lloyd-Jones: *The Fight of Faith, 1939–1981.* The Banner of Truth Trust (Edinburgh, 1990).

Murray, 1994: Murray, I.H. *D. Martyn Lloyd-Jones. Letters, 1919–1981.* The Banner of Truth Trust (Edinburgh, 1994).

Lloyd-Jones Archive: The National Library of Wales, Aberystwyth. D.M. & Mrs Lloyd-Jones, Letters and Papers in the Lloyd-Jones Archives: Cyfeirnod 29, 60–61, 63–65, 63–72, 66, 67, 68, 69, 70, 72.

The National Library of Wales, Phillips: The National Library of Wales, Aberystwyth: Dictionary of Welsh Biography. Phillips, Evan (1829–1912).

Ray, 2006: Ray, C. *Morning Devotions by Susannah Spurgeon: Free Grace and Dying Love. Including the Life of Sussanah Spurgeon* by Charles Ray. The Banner of Truth Trust (Edinburgh, 2006).

Rubython, 2011: Rubython, T. *And God Created Burton.* The Myrtle Press (Great Britain, 2011).

Schaeffer, 1976: Schaeffer, E. *What is a Family?* Hodder and Stoughton (London, 1976).

Shenton, 2001: Shenton, T. *Christmas Evans: The Life and Times of the One-eyed preacher of Wales.* Evangelical Press (Darlington, 2001).

Smellie, A. *Men of the Covenant.* The Banner of Truth Trust (Edinburgh, 1960).

Spurgeon, C.H. *Autobiography: 1. The Early Years.* The Banner of Truth Trust (Edinburgh, 1962).

Ten Boom, 1985: Ten Boom, C. *Jesus Is Victor.* Kingsway Publications Ltd. (Eastbourne, East Sussex, 1985).

Waters, 2006: Waters, G.P. *The Federal Vision and Covenant Theology: A Comparative Analysis.* Presbyterian & Reformed Publishing (Phillipsburg, New Jersey, 2006).

Williams, 1947: *Williams, Rev. H. The Romance of the Forward Movement of the Presbyterian Church of Wales.* Published for the author by Gee & Son (Denbigh, 1947).

Williams, 2003: Williams, W. *The Experience Meeting.* Regent College Publishing (This Edition Vancouver, 2003)..

NOT AGAINST
FLESH AND BLOOD

MARTYN LLOYD-JONES

ISBN 978-1-84550-735-0

Not Against Flesh and Blood

MARTIN LLOYD-JONES

The author reminds us that the devil operates on a worldwide scale as well as upon individuals. He traces the confusion and chaos of present-day society to the destructive work of satan and states that in a day where there is a renewed fascination with astrology, the occult, spiritism and 'doctrines of devils', to be aware of these evil powers, otherwise it will almost certainly mean that we will be defeated by them..

"This powerful volume, *Not Against Flesh and Blood*, is a prime example of the power and enduring relevance of The Doctor's ministry. It is robustly biblical, thoroughly orthodox, spiritually urgent, and theologically sound. Beyond these qualities, the book stands out for its brave and timely consideration of spiritual warfare – one of the most timely concerns in the present hour of Christianity."

R. Albert Mohler
President, The Southern Baptist Theological Seminary,
Louisville, Kentucky

THE PLIGHT
OF MAN
AND THE
POWER OF GOD

MARTYN LLOYD-JONES

ISBN 978-1-84550-736-7

The Plight of Man and the Power of God

MARTIN LLOYD-JONES

Martyn Lloyd-Jones' preaching always had an emphasis on the desperate plight of man and the power of God to save. His preaching was crystal clear on the sovereignty of God in the salvation of sinners, a concept that does not sit comfortably in our day of pragmatism, programmes and self-help books. Nevertheless it remains at the core of what the world needs to hear. Based on Romans chapter 1, this wonderful book will help you understand what the gospel is. As we live in a world that seems to be spiralling out of control, you will want to hear this message again and again.

> "We must rouse ourselves and realize afresh that though our Gospel is timeless and changeless, it nevertheless is always contemporary. We must meet the present situation and we must speak a word to the world that none else can speak."

Martyn Lloyd-Jones (1899-1981)
Martyn Lloyd-Jones was born in Wales and had a far-reaching influence through his ministry at Westminster Chapel in London, England from 1938-68.

> "What we have in these five expositions is the Gospel explained with great clarity and hope. Even today I used these timeless chapters with a non-Christian friend who is seeking to understand Christianity. I commend these messages to you."

Mark Dever
Senior Pastor, Capitol Hill Baptist Church and President, 9Marks.org, Washington, DC

Christian Focus Publications

Our mission statement –

STAYING FAITHFUL
In dependence upon God we seek to impact the world through literature faithful to His infallible Word, the Bible. Our aim is to ensure that the Lord Jesus Christ is presented as the only hope to obtain forgiveness of sin, live a useful life and look forward to heaven with Him.

Our books are published in four imprints:

CHRISTIAN FOCUS

Popular works including bi-ographies, commentaries, basic doctrine and Christian living.

CHRISTIAN HERITAGE

Books representing some of the best material from the rich heritage of the church.

MENTOR

Books written at a level suitable for Bible College and seminary students, pastors, and other seri-ous readers. The imprint includes commentaries, doctrinal studies, examination of current issues and church history.

CF4•K

Children's books for quality Bible teaching and for all age groups: Sunday school curriculum, puzzle and activity books; personal and family devotional titles, biographies and inspirational stories – because you are never too young to know Jesus!

Christian Focus Publications Ltd,
Geanies House, Fearn, Ross-shire,
IV20 1TW, Scotland, United Kingdom.
www.christianfocus.com
blog.christianfocus.com